A GUIDE TO OLIVE PESTS AND DISEASES

A GUIDE TO OLIVE PESTS AND DISEASES

Treating Olive Pests, Diseases and Disorders Worldwide, Growing 'Happy' Olive Trees and Reducing Reliance on Chemical Use

Vera Sergeeva

CONTENTS

ABOUT THE AUTHOR

Dr Vera Sergeeva is an international consultant in plant pathology, operates her own consultancy company OliVera in Australia, and promotes the Mediterranean diet.

She is well known in the Australian olive industry as an authority on pests and diseases of olives. She has collaborated in a number of research projects at Western Sydney University in Integrated Pest Management (IPM). Her research interests include biological and non-chemical plant protection and more environmentally friendly processes to grow olives.

Some research work was part of a project funded by Horticulture Australia Limited and Boundary Bend Management, Boort.

She was a convener of the Symposium on Plants, as Factories of Natural Substances, Edible and Essential Oils, organised by IHC2014 and WOCMAP, chairperson at the Olivebioteq 2014, 13th Congress of the Mediterranean Phytopathological Union and IOBC/WPRS working group on integrated protection of olive crop conferences. Dr Sergeeva is a certified olive oil taster and has been invited to be a judge at the Sydney Fine Food Show.

Dr Sergeeva contributed two chapters – 'Following Olive Footprints in Australia' and 'Following Olive Footprints in New Zealand' – to the 2012 book *Following Olive Footprints* (Olea europapaea L.) – *Cultivation and Culture, Folklore and History, Tradition and Uses*, which was a joint publication between AARINENA, IOC and ISHS.

She wrote the chapter 'Olive Diseases and Disorders in Australia and New Zealand' in the book *Olive Diseases and Disorders* (Research Signpost, 2012) and the chapter 'Medicinal Plants to Control Diseases and Pests' in the book *Medicinal and Aromatic Plants of the World* (Research Signpost, 2015).

Since the year 2000 Dr Sergeeva has visited olive groves in Australia, New Zealand, Spain, Portugal, Italy, Greece, Argentina, Chile, Japan, Jordan, Israel, Croatia and Montenegro. She has presented papers of olive diseases at national and international conferences and published more than 40 articles in refereed scientific and industry journals. She has visited olive groves in Australia on a regular basis for identifying disease problems, and participated in National Olive Industry Conferences and Workshops.

ABOUT THIS GUIDE

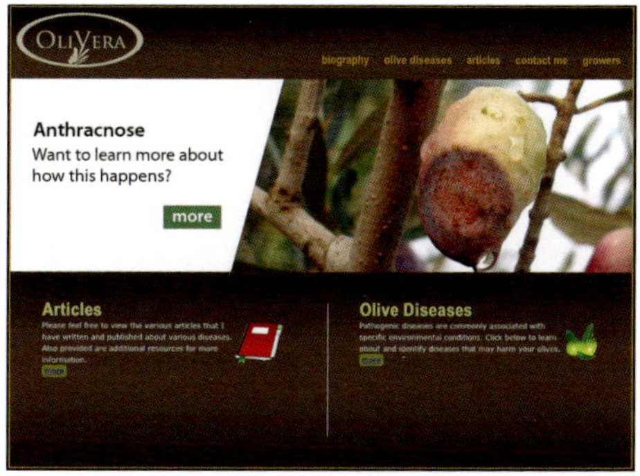

Olives are now one of the most extensively cultivated fruit crops in the world. The OliVera website was developed in 2010 online by Dr Sergeeva, providing information and assistance to olive growers on identification and the management of olive pests and diseases. Olive cultivation faces **more than 100 pests and pathogens which infect olive trees, reducing yields and increasing total production costs**. As a result of the success of the website, olive growers asked Dr Sergeeva to publish this fully up-to-date *A Guide to Olive Pests and Diseases*.

Due to the growth of the industry it has become even more important to address the issues of product quality and the adoption of Integrated Pest and Disease Management (IPDM). The correct identification of pests, beneficials, diseases and disorders is a fundamental part of IPDM, which is a common-sense approach to minimising crop damage by pests and diseases. It uses a number of simultaneously applied control methods which, collectively, discourage pests and diseases and encourage beneficial organisms, leading to a more balanced crop ecosystem that improves the quality of olive fruits with minimal adverse effects to the environment.

A Guide to Olive Pests and Diseases is designed to assist olive growers, agronomists, students, research scientists, diagnostic laboratories and consultants to correctly identify pests, diseases and non-pathogenic disorders such as weather damage and climate stress that may harm olives worldwide. It contains a comprehensive list of pests, diseases and disorders identified as currently important to olive industry. The information it contains is relevant in all olive-growing countries. The assessment of olive-tree health has always relied on a careful study of symptoms. Since symptoms are often the only evidence available for diagnosis, their recognition and interpretation are the key elements of this guide.

Introduction

The cultivated olive tree (*Olea europaea* L. subsp. *europaea* var. *europaea*; Oleaceae: Lamiales) is one of the world's most extensively grown fruit-tree crops, with an important economic role especially in Mediterranean countries. The oil, fruit, and leaves of the olive tree have an ancient history of nutritional, medicinal and traditional uses. It is an emblematic species owing to its ecological, economic and cultural importance.

In the last 20–30 years, interest in olive oil production and consumption has expanded olive cultivation to regions and countries outside the Mediterranean Basin, including Australia, New Zealand, South Africa, China, India, South America and the USA.

According to International Olive Growing Worldwide Analysis and Summary, at present olive growing comprises an area of 11.5 million hectares (28.4 million acres) of olive trees in 58 countries on five continents, with the products derived from this activity – olive oil and table olives – consumed in 179 countries. There is also the possibility of growing productive olive trees in other countries, which will surely expand the present area: in such locations in the United Kingdom, where 5 ha (12 acres) have been planted; Canada, where there is a farm of 3 ha (7 acres) producing table olives; and Nepal, where there have been several fruitful studies on this crop.

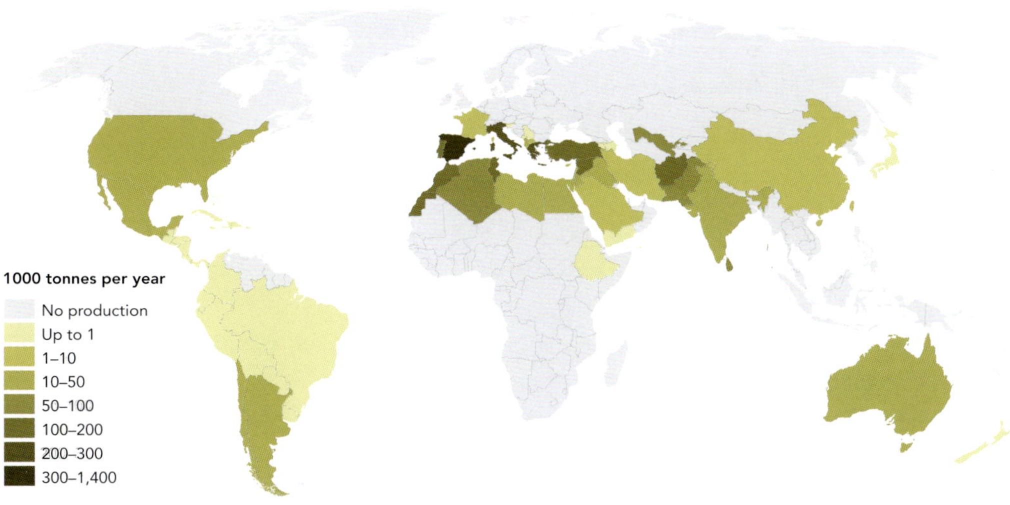

World production of olive oil from 2020–23. (SOURCE: INTERNATIONAL OLIVE COUNCIL)

Olives are now one of the most extensively cultivated fruit crops in the world. **Unfortunately, olive trees are prone to attack from a variety of pathogens and pests, which affect their health, yield and oil quality. More than 100 pests and pathogens infect olive trees, reducing yields and increasing total production costs.**

The trends developed in the second half of the 20th century – to have a chemical solution for every issue, be it fertility or disease – are today understood to be flawed. Chemicals have their role but today it is understood that they must be used empathetically with the environment and the ecology of a location.

Olive growers are asking: How to grow a healthy crop? Why are olive trees dying? When is the crop most susceptible to pest damage? When is the crop under stress? What are the reasons that an olive tree has yellow leaves? And many other questions. Most growers have difficulty in correctly identifying diseases and disorders such as anthracnose, cercosporiose, chilling, frost damage and water stress because symptoms can look similar. This book aims to answer those questions and facilitate the growth of healthy olive trees and crops.

Olive tree health

'Happy trees are healthy trees' and tree health starts with how the nursery cares for and attends to its new trees. The first thing to notice is a tree's general appearance. A healthy tree will have the following traits.

Signs of a healthy tree

- Nice overall look.
- Lack of abnormal symptoms in foliage or growth.
- No dead branches and twigs.
- No abnormal shoots, shortened internodes and proliferation.
- No signs of nutrient deficiency or root rot disorders such as brown leaves.
- No scarring on the trunk and branches.
- Absence of blotching or holes on leaves that indicate insects or diseases.
- Uniform bark that's not wounded or blemished.
- Well-developed top leader – the vertical stem located at the top of the trunk.
- Trunks that taper uniformly.
- What's even more important to consider is what's going on below ground in the root system. Roots are crucial because they anchor the tree and provide nutrient- and water-passage from the soil to the tree.

Assessing the health of an olive tree depends on the study of all factors (biotic and abiotic) affecting the vigour and productivity of the tree. Different types of damage can be expressed qualitatively by describing the symptoms, or quantitatively through assessment of crown condition. The health problems of a tree can be divided into: (a) diseases caused by pathogens, (b) damage by insect pests or animals, and (c) disorders. More than one factor can affect the health of a tree at any one time, and differentiation can be made between the primary disease/pest, which first and foremost affects the health of the tree, and the secondary disease/pest, which has a less important influence and usually affects trees already weakened by an existing factor.

Stress and off-site factors have a major role in determining the health or condition of trees, as do poor soil and irrigation.

> An especially important concept is that olive-tree care attempts to manage plant health rather than just control pest problems.

Due to the growth of the olive industry it has become even more important to address the issues of product quality and the adoption of integrated pest and disease management (IPDM). Tree health and vigour can be massively improved over time by balanced nurturing and integrated pest and disease management (IPDM). A proper understanding of climate, soils and grove management are vitally important to the nurturing of trees, which affects health, quality and yield.

- Healthy, productive plants can use their natural defence systems to resist environmental stresses.
- As a result, they need less chemical input for survival and productive long-term growth.
- The sensible approach to pest control is to create a natural balance of organisms in an olive grove. In a diverse ecosystem, pest populations are naturally regulated. Development of this balance relies on using products that minimise harm to beneficial organisms.

When is a tree unhealthy?

The answer is when symptoms are observed in the crown, on the foliage, or on stems (shoots, branches or trunks). The impracticality of examining tree roots means that many fail to do so, and this may mask important evidence, but for serious problems symptoms are usually manifest in other parts of the tree. The detection of ill health depends on the initial recognition of symptoms. Some symptoms are easy to identify, for example wilted leaves and stems with cankers, but others are not and may be difficult to distinguish from events that occur in the normal cycle of growth.

Some warning signs to look for are:

- Insects visible on the tree
- Brown lesions causing rot on fruit visible on the tree
- Lack of fruit or flowers
- Distortions in leaf size, colour or shape
- Holes in bark, branches or leaves
- Growths on branches
- Oozing sap
- Slowing in growth rate
- Wilting

Pests and disease outbreaks may indicate that your olive grove is under stress, for example from humid weather, water stress, soil-nutrient deficiencies, a tree canopy that's out of control, low numbers of natural beneficial organisms, and so on.

Pest insects, nematodes, termites and the microorganisms that cause plant disease only become 'pests and diseases' when their activities start to damage the trees. However, it is unwise to eradicate them altogether, as they also have a role to play in the natural ecosystem.

Pathogenic diseases are commonly associated with specific environmental conditions. In addition, non-pathogenic disorders, such as damage by heat and sun, wind, rain, fire, moisture, temperature, sunlight and other weather conditions can cause sunburn, russet, leaf scorch, pit burn, shrivelling, frost, chilling, hail injuries, water stress and nutrient deficiency, all of which interfere with the normal physiological processes in trees. These can be directly caused by environmental conditions and can negatively impact on pollination, reduced crop set, yield, slow tree decline and dieback. If one of these factors is out of balance it may lead to environmental stress, which may in turn result in a greater tendency for a tree to become diseased.

Climate change and pests and diseases

Climate change can affect the population size, survival rate and geographical distribution of pests; and the intensity, development and geographical distribution of diseases. Several pathogens, insects and nematodes affect olive trees, threatening olive production. The number of these occurrences has dramatically increased in recent years, causing serious damage to olive production.

What environmental factors affect olive tree health?

The environment is usually the factor that controls whether disease develops or not. Environmental conditions may determine the presence of the pathogen in a particular season through their effects on processes such as overwintering. Environmental conditions also affect the ability of the pathogen to cause disease.

Simply put, plant disease will not occur if there is no viable pathogen, or no susceptible host plant, or the environmental conditions are not favourable. If any one of the three factors is missing, the triangle is not complete and no disease will occur. The severity of disease depends on the favourable level of each factor. How susceptible is the plant? How virulent is the pathogen? How conducive are the existing environmental conditions in supporting disease and pathogen spread?

Approximately 50 million olive trees are under irrigation, but dryland crops dominate. Global climate change, especially global warming, is affecting olive production efficiency as well as its product quality.

Each pest and disease species will respond differently to a warmer and drier climate, and it helps to gain an understanding of the species likely to act as entry points for fungal rots such as anthracnose, which then destroy the crop.

Once a pest or disease has started to attack a crop, the damage cannot be repaired and control becomes increasingly difficult. Where possible, it is preferable to use techniques to avoid or prevent pest and disease attack in the first place. Environmental factors play an important role in managing pests, diseases and disorders.

Regional climate levels:

- *Macroclimate refers to the general weather pattern in the region. It is difficult to control or cannot be managed, and is unpredictable.
- *Mesoclimate refers to the climate in the area where the crops are grown. It is difficult to control, can be measured but cannot be managed easily. Planting tree breaks can sometimes change the mesoclimate.
- *Microclimate refers to the climate within and immediately surrounding the crops. This can be controlled through cultural practices such as opening up the canopy and regulating irrigation.

CHAPTER 1

Pests

Insect Pests

Order Diptera: Flies

Fruit flies [Diptera: Tephritidae]

- **Olive fruit fly** *Bactrocera oleae* (Rossi, 1790)

Geographical distribution: Worldwide, excluding Australia and New Zealand. One of the most damaging insect pests of olives.

- **Mediterranean fruit fly** *Ceratitis capitata* (Wied, 1824)

Geographical distribution: Worldwide.

- **Queensland fruit fly** *Bactrocera tryoni* (Froggatt, 1897)

Geographical distribution: Australia.

Olive fruit fly *Bactrocera oleae*

Damage: fruits.

Morphology: Adult 5mm (0.2in) long, brown abdomen with black markings along the sides, although the colouring varies greatly. Eggs white, elongated, 0.8mm (0.03in) long. Three larval instars and one pupal stage. Several generations – four or five occur through the year. The actual number is closely linked to the climate and to the availability of olive fruits.

Life cycle: Adults and larvae (maggots) overwinter in fruit on the tree while the pupae do so in the soil. The start of the first summer generation depends on fruit susceptibility and temperature conditions. Between three and four generations can occur from early autumn until winter. The female can lay up to 20 eggs per day on the fruits, producing several hundred eggs during her lifespan. Fruits are damaged by the egg laying. The larvae feed within the fruit mesocarp, damaging it and diminishing its quality. They can also induce premature fruit ripening or fall. In addition, the skin puncture marks allow entry of fungal rots, such as anthracnose. Fruit flies have the potential to spread the fungus in olives, as well as in other crops. The factors contributing to the economic losses caused by the olive fruit fly include direct damage through fruit drop and weight loss, and indirect damage due to the poor quality of the oils produced in infested areas. The loss in oil quality is caused by the development of microflora inside the galleries made by the larvae.

Economic importance: Olive fruit fly causes serious economic damage. It is one of the most damaging and devastating olive-tree pests in the Mediterranean basin. Damage caused by this fruit fly can reduce production by 50–60 per cent, causing large losses in olive oil production.

Olive fruit fly, *Bactrocera oleae*.
(MARSHALL JOHNSON)

Damage to fruit caused by olive fruit fly.

Damage to fruit caused by olive fruit fly.

Queensland fruit fly larva and pupa on olive fruit.

Olive leaf gall midge

Dasineura oleae (Angelini, 1831) = *Perrisia oleae* [Diptera: Cecidomyiidae]

Geographical distribution: Mediterranean region.
Damage: Leaves, vegetative buds, flower stalks and stems.
Morphology: Adult 5mm (0.2in) long. Female fertility approx. 100 eggs. Egg elongated, slightly tapering at each end, pale yellow in colour, turning to red at both ends. Larva yellow with dark brown bilobate sternal plate. Pupa orange-red.
Larvae cause slight, indefinite, elongate swellings (galls) on olive leaves. Per gall, only one larva develops. Infestation of the stalks may additionally lead to yield loss. Galls induced in these tissues interrupt the nutrient flow to the growing fruits, and small-sized fruits are produced.
Economic importance: Considered a secondary pest. However, severe outbreaks have been recorded in the Mediterranean Basin, causing reduction in the yield.

Damage to leaves caused by olive leaf gall midge. (A. SANCHIONI)

Olive fruit midge

Lasioptera berlesiana (Paoli, 1907) = *Prolasioptera berlesiana, L. brevicornis* [Diptera-Cecidomylidae]

Geographical distribution: Mediterranean region.
Damage: Fruits.
Morphology: Adults about 1.5mm (0.06in) long, generally brown with abdomen paler and dark spots on the dorsum of third to seventh uromeres.

Larva red or reddish, with a bifurcate sternal spatula anteriorly, and 2mm (0.08in) long when fully grown. Pupa 2mm (0.08in) long, at first dark red and later dark brown. Olive fruit midge is a parasitoid of olive fruit fly. The midge larva lives in the tunnels made in the fruits by the larva of the fly. In these tunnels also lives the fungus *Camarosporium dalmaticum*.

According to some sources the midge larva lives as a mycophage on this fungus; others state that it is a predator on the fly larvae.
Economic importance: This midge is considered harmful because it favours the establishment of *C. dalmaticum* fungus in olives.

Olive bark midge / Olive shoot midge

Resseliella oleisuga (Targioni-Tozzetti, 1887) [Diptera: Cecidomyiidae]

Geographical distribution: Widely distributed.
Damage: Woody stems, bark.
Morphology: Adult 3mm (0.1in) long, black, with orange (female) and greyish (male) abdominal segments. Egg 0.3mm (0.01in) long, elliptic, elongated; initially transparent, turning to yellow prior to hatching. Larva 3–4mm (0.1–0.2in) long, initially transparent, later turning whitish and then orange in later stages. Pupa 1.5–2.2mm (0.06–0.09in) long, dark yellow or orangish. Small clusters of 10–30 eggs laid under damaged bark. Larvae develop under the bark and feed on the cambium. They cause necrosis of the bark around the oviposition site and then dried shoots and dead branches.
Economic importance: A pest of potential economic importance.

Olive bark midge, *Resseliella oleisuga* – late-stage larva and its appearance under the bark. (AZIZ ÖZKAN)

Resseliella oleisuga adult. (ASSOPROLI BARI AGRICOLA)

Order Lepidoptera: Moths

Olive Moth

Prays oleae (Bernard, 1788) [Lepidoptera: Yponomeutidae]

Geographical distribution: Widespread through Mediterranean Basin.
Damage: Leaves, terminal buds, flowers and fruits.
Morphology: Adult 6.5mm (0.25in) long with wingspan of about 13mm (0.5in). Egg sub-ovate, convex, very reticular. White when recently laid, then turning yellowish during development. Sensitive to increases in temperature and decreases in humidity. Five larval instars. Pupa enclosed in a dirty white, loosely knit silk cocoon. Three generations occur annually. The first generation lives and develops on the flower buds and flowers, the second generation lives on the fruit with the larvae developing inside the fruit and damaging the kernel (known as 'kernel borer'), and the third generation develops on the leaves (known as 'leaf miner'). The damage caused by the first generation is a reduced yield when infestation is serious. The second generation can cause real damage and economic loss.
Economic importance: One of the most damaging and devastating olive tree pests in the Mediterranean basin. Damage caused by this moth can reduce production by 50–60 per cent, causing significant losses in olive oil production.

Leaf miner larva feeding on leaves.

Fruit damage caused by larvae. (BIOCHEMTECH)

Olive spinner moth

Zelleria oleastrella (Milliere, 1864) [Lepidoptera: Yponomeutidae]

Geographical distribution: North Africa, Middle East, Turkey and Europe.
Damage: Twigs and leaves infested with larvae and pupae.
Morphology: Adult wingspan 11–15 mm (0.4–0.6in). Larvae usually bore into terminal buds of host plant, but may also inhabit the tips of young shoots. Pupation takes place beneath a slight silken web.
Economic importance: The damage to olives is negligible.

Zelleria oleastrella adult. (FRIEDMAR GRAF)

Larva feeding in a slight web on the shoots. (MEERT RUBEN)

Olive pyralid moth

Euzophera pinguis (Haworth, 1811) [Lepidoptera: Pyralidae]

Geographical distribution: Mediterranean region.
Damage: Feeds on bark and wood, damaging sap flows and weakening the olive trees.
Morphology: Adult 13mm (0.5in) long with a wingspan of 20–25mm (0.8–1in), beige to dark brown in colour. Forewings marked with two pale zigzag lines. Eggs are flattened oval shape. The larval galleries damage the plant vessels and block sap

Adult pyralid moth.

Damage caused by larva. (OLIVICOLTORI SESTRESI)

Damage by larva. (N. GANDOLFO)

circulation. This causes pronounced vegetative decline in the olive grove, apparent in the intense yellow colour of most of the infested branches. Severe leaf loss ensues and the branch may die. Diagnosis is easy since the sawdust produced by the larvae as they dig their galleries can be seen on the infested branches. Another typical symptom is a swelling at the points on the infested branches where sap retention occurs. Damage can by very serious in young orchards, and in extreme cases the whole tree may be lost.

Economic importance: A serious bark- and wood-borer olive pest in most Mediterranean regions.

Palpita moth / Jasmine moth

Palpita unionalis (Hübner, 1796) = *Palpita vitrealis* (Rossi, 1794) = *Margaronia unionalis* (Hb) = [Lepidoptera: Pyralidae]

Geographical distribution: Europe, Asia and Algeria.

Damage: Leaves, terminal buds and fruits.

Morphology: Adult wingspan 30mm (1.2in), satiny white colour. Egg: whitish in colour. Six larval stages. When hatched, the young larva is yellowish as it develops it turns greenish. When fully developed, the larva is 18–25mm (0.7–1in) long and spins a silk cocoon among the leaves where it metamorphoses into a pupa. Mainly nocturnal. Has various generations through the year. The larvae cause damage by feeding on the leaves, shoots, terminal buds and fruits.

Economic importance: A dangerous pest, attacking sapling olive trees and nurseries, tender shoots and ripening fruits, inducing economic losses. If fruit is affected by high densities of larvae, the damage can be serious.

Olive leaf moth

Palpita forficifera (Munroe, 1959) [Lepidoptera: Crambidae]

Geographical distribution: Brazil and Uruguay (native to South America).
Damage: Leaves, buds and fruits.
The principal pest in olive groves in Brazil and Uruguay can cause severe yield losses if not managed properly. The eggs are found in olive branches and leaves. Damage caused by the caterpillars is due to feeding on tender buds, compromising production in the following year. Based on the thermal requirements, *P. forficifera* can produce four to six generations per year in olive-producing regions. While feeding, the larvae form webs over the leaves, causing them to close. This ecological relationship between insect and plant may provide an adequate microclimate that allows the moth to survive through critical periods of its development, especially during cold seasons.
Economic importance: The caterpillar is the main pest of olive trees.

Olive leaf moth / Olive shootworm

Palpita persimilis (Munroe, 1959) [Lepidoptera: Crambidae]

Geographical distribution: North America, Brazil and Uruguay.
Damage: Leaves and shoots.
The larvae can cause defoliation of new growth. The larvae tie leaves together with silk to make nests on shoot tips. Feeding damage can be just on the epidermis of the leaf, or as larvae age they will chew holes in leaves.
Economic importance: The caterpillar is a potential pest.

Jasmine moth and Lilac pyralid moth

Palpita vitrealis and *Palpita nigropunctalis* (Bremer, 1864) [Lepidoptera: Crambidae]

Geographical distribution: *Palpita vitrealis* widespread in Eurasia, Africa and Australia. *P. nigropunctalis* in East Asia – feeds on several oleaceous species. The larvae commonly construct untidy webs of leaves and silk in which they consume the leaves and, in some species, also the fruit.

Adult jasmine moth, *Palpita vitrealis*. (ANNETTE HERZ)

Pupa of jasmine moth in a leaf coil with silken cocoon opened. (ANNETTE HERZ)

Young larvae of jasmine moth feeding on lower surface of olive leaf. (ANNETTE HERZ)

Damage to olive fruit caused by larva of jasmine moth. (ANNETTE HERZ)

Damage caused by jasmine moth larva.

Light brown apple moth

Epiphyas postvittana (Walker, 1863) [Lepidoptera: Tortricidae]

Geographical distribution: Australia, New Zealand and California (USA).

Damage: Leaves.

Morphology: Adult wingspan 18mm (0.7in). The moth is typically yellow-brown overall and has dark markings on the forewings. Larvae are generally yellowish-green and may vary according to instar and host. Final-instar larvae are 10–20mm (0.4–0.8in) in length. This moth is a species of leafroller with a wide range of host plants. It damages growing tips or inflorescences of olives, tying them together with silken threads to form a protected area within which it feeds.

Economic importance: Rare, but can occur in young olive trees in grape-growing areas.

Adult.

Early-instar larva.

Pupa in silken threads on olive.

Larva damage on olive.

Tortricid moth

Argyrotaenia sphaleropa (Meyrick, 1909) [Lepidoptera: Tortricidae]

Geographical distribution: Brazil and Uruguay (native to South America).
Damage: Leaves and buds.
Morphology: Adult wingspan 15mm (0.6in) for female and 12mm (0.5in) for male. Female lays eggs in masses on leaves – when larvae emerge they disperse in search of suitable feeding sites. They cause harm through the consumption of the plant tissue of young leaves and buds, scraping the skin of the fruit and leaves, reducing photosynthetic capacity and fruit quality. This moth is a native species with polyphagous habits.
Economic importance: Has the potential to occasionally reach the status of pest.

European Grapevine moth

Lobesia botrana (Denis and Schiff, 1776) [Lepidoptera: Tortricidae]

Geographical distribution: Europe South and America.
Damage: Leaves, occasionally on the flowers of olive.
Morphology: Adult wingspan 6mm (0.25in); forewings are cream-white with grey, black and brown markings; hindwings are white (male) or dark grey (female). Adults feed on nectar. Final-instar larvae are 10–15mm (0.4–0.6in) long and vary from light yellowish-green to pale brown. Larvae spin silken webs to tie leaves or inflorescences. Overwinters as a pupa at various locations, such as under leaf litter, in soil and under grapevine bark. Pupa 6mm (0.25in) long, brown. Primarily a pest on the flowers and fruit of grapevines, but has been known to infest stone-fruit trees and olives.
Economic importance: The damage caused by this moth to olives is negligible.

European grapevine moth. (SEDQ)

Rustic sphinx moth

Manduca rustica (Fabricius, 1775) [Lepidoptera: Sphingidae]

Geographical distribution: Florida (USA).
Damage: Leaves.
Morphology: Adult 87–150mm (3.4–5.9in) long, with heavy body. Usually nocturnal, feeding late at night. Moths in this family are called hawkmoths and the caterpillars are often referred to as hornworms, due to the horn-shaped protuberance found on their posterior end. Tends to make pupal cases in small gaps in the soil, making them easy to accidentally transport and difficult to find on purpose. Larvae cause defoliation of olive trees in Florida – a single larva can quickly denude a two-year-old olive tree, causing problems for nursery producers and for growers with new plantings. Although trees can recover from this damage, olive trees are slow growing, and feeding damage can remain apparent for several months depending on the time of year. Many growers report success in removing these pests by hand.
Economic importance: An occasional pest for olives in Florida.

Adult Rustic sphinx moth. (LYLE J. BUSS, UNIVERSITY OF FLORIDA)

Caterpillars are also known as 'hornworms'. (B. GIBBONS)

Death's-head hawkmoth

Acherontia atropos (Linnaeus, 1758) [Lepidoptera: Sphingidae]

Geographical distribution: Europe, North Africa and Middle East.
Damage: Leaves.
Morphology: Adult wingspan 130mm (5.1in). A powerful flier. Forewings mottled dark brown and pale brown, and hindwings are orange-buff with two narrow dark bands parallel with the hind margin. The abdomen is a similar orange-brown, with a broad, dark dorsal stripe.

Caterpillar. (OLIVICOLTURA ITALIANA)

Larva up to 130mm (5.1in) in length, its colouration varying according to its host plants, being yellow, green or brown, with diagonal blue stripes and five pairs of prolegs. Larvae are leaf feeders, usually with a posterior tail-like scolus. Host plants recorded in numerous plant families. A few are of economic significance, although in 1976 there was an outbreak on olive trees in Greece. Females emerge in spring and place single eggs on host plants, which are eaten by the larvae. Towards autumn they descent to the soil to pupate, thus raising only a single generation each year.
Economic importance: An occasional pest for olives in Greece and Italy.

Caterpillar feeding on olive leaves.

Leopard moth / Wood-borer moth

Zeuzera pyrina (Linnaeus, 1761) [Lepidoptera: Cossidae]

Geographical distribution: Mediterranean Region, Egypt.
Damage: Leaf petioles, young twigs, twigs, branches and trunk.
Morphology: Adults have 50–70mm (2–2.8in) wingspan for female and 40–50mm (1.6–2in) for male. White, speckled with numerous large dark blue spots on the forewings and paler dots on the hindwings. Egg approx. 1mm (0.04in), oval, subelliptic in shape and yellow to salmon in colour; often laid in clusters in bark cracks or in old galleries.

Five larval instars, followed by a pupal stage. By the end of development the larva can be 50–60mm (2–2.4in) long. Pupa 35mm (1.4in) long, yellowish-brown in colour. Pupation takes place at the entrance to the larval gallery, which is plugged with sawdust. The larvae attack the young shoots on the outer part of the tree, which they penetrate by digging upward galleries under the bark.
Economic importance: A dangerous wood-borer and the most serious and devastating threat to olive trees.

Adult moth. (ANTROPOCENEIT)

Caterpillar. (ANTROPOCENEIT)

Damage caused by larva. (DAVID BRACEY)

Order Coleoptera: Beetles

Olive fruit curculio / Olive fruit weevil

Rhynchites cribripennis (Desbrochers,1869) [Coleoptera: Attelabidae]

Geographical distribution: Mediterranean Region and Middle East.
Damage: Leaves and fruits.
Morphology: Adult red to reddish-brown, except for black abdomen and mandibles. Body length including rostrum is 5.5–6 mm (0.2–0.24in). Adults drill holes in the flesh of olives, resulting in fruit drop. The overwintered adults emerge from the soil in spring and fly to olive trees, feeding initially on leaves and shoots, later moving to the fruits. During summer the female bores a hole in a fruit and places an egg there. The larva feeds on the seed, devouring it completely. In autumn the grown larva drops to the upper soil layers, where it remains in diapause until the following summer. It pupates in early autumn and the adult emerges in spring. Economic damage, especially in the early stages of fruit formation, is caused by fruit puncturing for oviposition and by larval feeding. This can lead to early fruit drop. Cultivars with small fruit are more seriously affected.
Economic importance: Considered to be of high importance as the damage can directly affect the quality of fruit.

Adult olive fruit curculio. (G. SELJAK)

Adult and the damage it has caused to olive fruits. (D. PERDIKIS, AGRICULTURAL UNIVERSITY OF ATHENS)

Olive borer / Olive bark beetle / Barrenillo negro

Hylesinus oleiperda (Fabricius, 1792) [Coleoptera: Scolytidae]

Geographical distribution: Mediterranean Region, South America and Japan.

Damage: Twigs.

Morphology: Adult is a small beetle, 3mm (0.12in) long, dark brown with elytra longitudinally striated, and showing marked convexity in lateral view. The cream-coloured larva is apodous, with dark brown mandibles. Different larval stages can be found for months in infested wood. The larva reaches a maximum length of 4mm (0.16in) and the pupa is slightly smaller and progressively shows the development of locomotor appendages, elytra and antennae. This species causes damage mainly in spring. During severe attacks, a large number of twigs are observed that initially show withered foliage, then later dry up completely, with the consequent loss of flower buds and flowers. This symptom can be confused with diseases such as Verticillium wilt. Olive borers overwinter as larva and have one generation per year.

Economic importance: A pest of potential economic importance.

Olive borer damage in areas of Jaén and Granada, Spain. (AGROES.ES)

Apple weevil

Otiorhynchus cribricollis (Gyllenhal, 1834) [Coleoptera: Curculionidae]

Geographical distribution: Mediterranean Region, California, New Zealand and Australia.

Damage: Leaf stalks, buds and fruit stems.

Morphology: Adult 9mm (0.35in) long, brown with a slightly bulbous abdomen. Overwinter as larvae, which go through 10 stages until development is

Apple weevil, *Otiorhynchus cribricollis*. (DAFWA)

completed at the beginning of spring.

During the day this beetle burrows into the ground underneath the olive tree. At night it climbs up to the crown and eats the leaves, leaving very characteristic marks with a notched appearance. Also feeds on soft bark, growing tips and fruit stalks. Young trees may be killed and mature trees have reduced yield.

In groves with high weevil numbers, fruit loss could be high as the season progresses.
Economic importance: A pest of potential economic importance.

Damage to leaves by apple weevil.

Garden weevil

Phlyctinus callosus (Boheman, 1834) [Coleoptera: Curculionidae]

Geographical distribution: South Africa (native), New Zealand and Australia (introduced, mainly in Western Australia).
Damage: Leaves and roots.
Morphology: Adult 7mm (0.28in) long, mainly dull grey-brown with some white speckling on the elytra. The antennae are long, almost equal to the length of one of the legs. There's also a concave, white, speckly stripe towards the posterior of the abdomen. Legless larva creamy-white with orange-brown head, growing to around 6mm (0.24in) in length. Pupa roughly 8mm (0.32in) long and covered in hooked bristles. Adult nocturnal and flightless; climbs trees to chew leaf margins. Severe infestations can damage growing tips, especially in young trees. The soil-dwelling larvae (legless grubs) may damage tree roots. Has one or two generations per year.
Economic importance: A pest of potential economic importance.

Olive weevil

Dyscerus perforatus (Roelofs, 1873) [Coleoptera; Curculionidae]

Geographical distribution: Japan (native).
Damage: Bark and trunk.
Morphology: The most serious insect pest for olives in Japan. Once the insects begin to infest olive trees, they increase their population very rapidly and the trees subsequently die. The females have a long egg-laying period from spring to autumn, and the larvae attack the bark and trunk of olive trees, weakening and

Dyscerus perforatus weevil damage to olives in Japan.

Olive weevil.

withering even adult trees as the assault progresses.

Economic importance: A pest of potential economic importance in Japan.

Olive bark beetle

Phleotribus scarabeoides (Bernard, 1788) [Coleoptera: Curculionidae]

Geographical distribution: Mediterranean Basin, including Europe, North Africa and parts of Asia.

Damage: Twigs, bark and leaves.

Adult olive borer, *Phloeotribus scarabaeoides*. (AGRARAOLIEARUM)

Borer entry holes. (SANCHEZ)

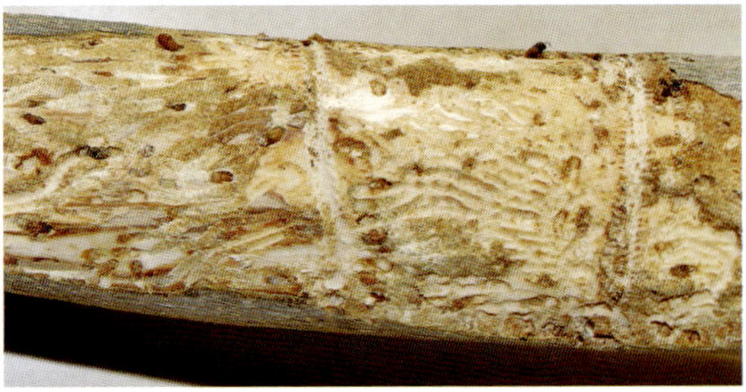

Olive bark beetle galleries. (MICHAEL HADJICONSTANTIS)

Morphology: Adult 2–2.5 mm (0.08–0.1in) long with a dark brown cylindrical body. Apodous larva about 3mm (0.12in) long and yellowish-white with brown head. Adult females bore through bark and excavate a transverse tunnel on either side of the entry point. Inside the twig/branch, the female lays up to 60 eggs and as they hatch each larva bores up or down from the entrance tunnel underneath the bark. This activity produces sawdust in the entrance hole. This feeding causes partial to complete girdling of the twig/branch; thereby structurally weakening it as well as damaging vasculature. Larvae pupate inside the feeding galleries. Has two to four generations per year.

Economic importance: A pest of potential economic importance.

South American fruit tree weevil

Naupactus xanthographus (Germar, 1824) [Coleoptera: Curculionidae]

South American fruit tree weevil. (LUCAS RUBIO)

Geographical distribution: Chile.

Damage: Roots and leaves.

Morphology: Adult female 14–18mm (0.55–0.7in) long; male smaller and narrower at 12–14mm (0.45–0.55in) long. Eggs oval, approximately 1mm (0.04in) long, yellow and laid under the bark in several clusters of 20–50. There are six larval stages and the final-stage larvae are up to 20mm (0.8in) long.

In olive orchards adults attack the roots, consuming a large quantity of rootlets and boring into larger roots, which affects the development of the plant and it can kill young plants and facilitate the development of root pathogens. Direct damage cause by larvae feeding on roots. Adult feeding causes superficial damage to leaves (irregular leaf margins).

Economic importance: The damage of these weevils to olives is negligible.

Fuller's rose weevil

Pantomorus cervinus (Boheman, 1840) [Coleoptera: Curculionidae]

Pantomorus cervinus adult. (ERNST)

Geographical distribution: Chile.
Damage: Leaves and roots.
Morphology: Adult wingless, grey-brown and about 8mm (0.3in) long. Mature larvae are legless, yellow and about 6mm (0.24in) long. Females produce 20–30 eggs glued together in yellowish, papery masses without mating. Eggs are laid under fruit calyces, in bark crevices or in micro-sprinklers under trees. After hatching, the larvae drop, burrow into the soil and feed on roots. Adults emerge from the soil mostly between February and May, but can be found all year round. There is one generation per year. The adults chew leaf margins, leaving a serrated edge. Foliage near the trunk or touching the ground is most likely to be damaged.
Economic importance: Causes negligible damage to olives.

Powderpost beetles / Tree wood-borers

Dexicrates robustus (Blanchard, 1851) and *Neoterius mystax* (Blanchard, 1851) [Coleoptera: Bostrychidae]

Dexicrates robustus adult. (JEAN-CYRILFREEMAN)

Geographical distribution: Chile.
Damage: Leaves and twigs.
Morphology These insects, clearly xylophagous, designed to drill, consume wood when they are adults, generating a large amount of very fine sawdust, which is an indication of their presence. The adult bores with its mouthparts, assisted by the pronotum, which is covered with tubercles that facilitate drilling into the wood. Adults and damage are usually detected during spring and early summer.
Economic importance: Adults occasionally capable of damaging healthy young trees in Chile.

Common auger beetle

Xylopsocus gibbicollis (MacLeay, 1873) [Coleoptera: Bostrichidae]

Geographical distribution: Australia (native).

Damage: Twigs.

Morphology: Adult 2mm (0.08in) long and 1mm (0.04in) wide, black/brown with a rounded head. The end of the adult's abdomen is flat, giving the appearance as if it has been sliced off. Adult beetles actively fly and this is the damaging stage of this insect. It does not feed on healthy conductive tissue of the wood of vines, but bores down into the wood.

Economic importance: Migrates into olive groves from nearby vineyards. The damage to olives is negligible.

Damage to olive twig caused by common auger beetle.

Common auger beetle adult.

Twig pruner

Cloniocerus kraussii (White, 1855) [Coleoptera: Cerambycidae]

Geographical distribution: South Africa (native).

Damage: Twigs.

Morphology: The beetle is a fairly hairy black, except for broad patches of buff on each side of the thorax. These longhorn borer beetles usually go for trees that are stressed, for example trees suffering water stress or trees stressed by diseases or soil-borne pests such as nematodes. These indigenous beetles attack plants in the family Oleaceae, including wild and cultivated olives. Larvae boring into younger shoots cause wilting or dieback.

Economic importance: A pest of potential economic importance.

Adult *Cloniocerus kraussii*.
(KOBUS.VISSER-49)

Olive flea beetles

Agropistes oleae (Bryant), *A. capensis* (Bryant) and *A. sexittatus* (Bryant) [Coleoptera: Cerambycidae]

Geographical distribution: South Africa (Western Cape).
Damage: Young growth, leaves and fruits.
Morphology: The beetles resemble ladybirds in shape and size. They are normally either yellow with black stripes or completely shiny black. When disturbed they have a habit of jumping instead of flying. They lay their yellow eggs underneath the leaves, sometimes covered with excrement. The larvae are leaf miners causing damage to young olive trees and more rarely to the olive fruit.
Economic importance: A pest of potential economic importance.

Agropistes oleae adult. (MAGRIETB)

Damage to leaves by olive flea beetles.

African black beetle

Heteronychus arator (F.) [Coleoptera: Scarabaeidae]

Geographical distribution: Africa (native), Australia (excluding Tasmania) and New Zealand (North Island).
Damage: Roots.
Morphology: Adults are 12mm (0.5in) long, oval in shape and shiny black; slow moving, usually found on or under soil surface. The root-feeding larvae, which are 35mm (1.4in) long when fully grown, cause most damage. The larval stage is present for only

Heteronychus arator adult.

Heteronychus arator larvae.

three to four months each year. Impact on newly planted olive trees has been noted only in Western Australia; there has been no observable impact on mature trees.

Economic importance: A pest of potential economic importance.

Cockchafer / White grub

Melolontha papposa (Illiger, 1803) [Coleoptera: Scarabaeidae]

Geographical distribution: Spain and Tunisia.

Damage: Roots and crown.

Morphology: Adult 15–19mm (0.6–0.8in) and varies from straw-coloured to dark brown. Larva white ('white grub'), reaches a very large 40mm (1.6in), are agile and 'aggressive' when handled. Larvae feed almost exclusively on olive roots, being virtually its only source of food in the

Melolontha papposa adult and larva. (PACO MORENO GÁMEZ)

olive grove. Level of damage to the olive roots depends on population level of the pest. The seedlings of young olive trees are more sensitive and may end up dying.

Economic importance: A pest of potential economic importance.

White-spotted rose beetle / Cetoniella

Oxythyrea funesta (Poda, 1761) [Coleoptera: Scarabaeidae]

White-spotted rose beetle on olive flowers in Italy. (ALESSIO CAMATTA)

Geographical distribution: Europe, Turkey and Middle East.

Damage: Flowers.

Morphology: Adult 6–12 mm (0.25–0.5in) long; more or less bronzed black, usually with six white spots in two longitudinal rows on the pronotum and many others on the elytra. Relatively long legs help the insect cling firmly to flowers. The head, which has a pair of powerful mandibles, is sclerified, as are the legs, to allow the insect to move more easily in the ground. This phytophagous insect feeds on pollen, but also gnaws at the floral organs, making it very harmful for agriculture, although paradoxically it plays an important role as pollinator. Damages mostly pale-coloured flowers and buds. 'C'-shaped larvae feed on plant roots and can remain in the soil until the following spring.

Economic importance: Damaging to buds and flowers; minor pest with no serious economic damage.

Blister beetle

Hycleus pustulatus (Thunberg, 1821) = *Mylabris pustulata* Olivier, 1795 [Coleoptera: Meloidae]

Geographical distribution: India, China.

Damage: Flowers.

Morphology: Body length about 14–33mm. Elytra pubescence is short, very dense on black area, but sparse on red area. Basal region has two reddish spots.

Economic importance: Caused extensive damage to olives at two localities in India. A phytophagous beetle that exhibits polyphagy. An economically significant species.

Blister beetle adult. (ARIAN SURESH)

Spanish fly

Lytta vesicatoria (Linnaeus, 1758) [Coleoptera: Meloidae]

Geographical distribution: Eurasia and North Africa.
Damage: Shoots, leaves and buds.
Morphology: Adult 15–20mm (0.6–0.8in) long. This aposematic emerald-green beetle has only one generation per year through a hypermetabolic cycle, where the females lay their eggs in the ground. Here the insect passes to the second larval stage. They pupate in spring, with the adults appearing en masse during June. Adults can live on olive trees, feeding on the leaves and potentially causing damage, especially to young plants where they irreparably damage the buds and compromise development. The beetles defoliate plants from top to bottom; moreover they can gnaw the axis of non-lignified shoots. The presence of this insect is perceptible through an intense smell similar to that of a mouse.
Economic importance: Minor pest with no serious economic damage.

Adult *Lytta vesicatoria* on an olive tree in Italy. (ANTONIO SIRIGNANO)

Order Thysanoptera: Thrips

Families and species found on olives include:

Family Aeolothripidae

- *Aeolothrips collaris* (Priesner, 1919)
- *Aeolothrips intermedius* (Bagnall, 1934)
- *Franklinothrips megalops* (Trybom, 1912)

Family Melanthripidae

- *Melanthrips fuscus* (Sulzer, 1776)

Family Thripidae

- *Frankliniella occidentalis* (Pergande, 1895)
- *Frankliniella schultzei* (Trybom, 1910)
- *Neohydatothrips amygdali* (Minaei, 2016)
- *Thrips imagines* (Bagnall, 1926)
- *Thrips tabaci* (Lindeman, 1889)

Family Phlaeothripidae

- *Haplothrips andresi* (Priesner, 1931)
- *Haplothrips tritici* (Kurdjumov, 1912)
- *Liothrips oleae* (Costa, 1857)

Geographic distribution: Widely distributed.

Damage: Flowers, leaves and fruits.

Morphology: Thrips are very small, slender insects with mouthparts specialised for sucking and rasping. Adults are 1–2mm (0.04–0.08in) long, and most have a pair of narrow wings fringed with long hairs. Juveniles are wingless and often paler than adults. Thrips are frequently associated with flowers, where they find different nutrients and oviposition sites. The nymph and adult stages feed by perforating the epidermis and sucking the contents of the cells, but they do not secrete honeydew or produce abundant sooty mould, although the large amount of faeces can eventually stain fruits. Their rasping-sucking mouth armour causes russet-type lesions. The damage can also manifest itself on the foliage. In addition, thrips lay eggs in fruits, which generates small skin lesions due to oviposition and the subsequent emergence of the nymphs. This may be more important in in terms of damage, as it affects the appearance of the fruit.

Economic importance: In general the damage caused by thrips is not very significant and is quite localised. However, in certain climatic and agronomic conditions damage may be considerable.

Olive fruits and leaves damaged by Western flower thrips, *Frankliniella occidentalis*.

Order Hemiptera: True Bugs

Scale Insects

Worldwide, olive trees host around 100 species of scale insects, approximately 43 per cent of which are found in the Mediterranean Basin.

Scale insects mostly have a waxy or armoured cover, which they use to protect themselves. There are two categories of scales – 'soft' and 'armoured' – and they can take various shapes. Most soft scales belong to the Coccidae, while the armoured scales belong to the Diaspididae.

The females of most species remain under cover for their entire life, while the male insects live under the covers until maturity, when they emerge as winged adults. Females are generally headless, legless and wingless, and when mature they produce eggs, then die. Most species of scale insects lay their eggs externally beneath the scale, although some species form a cyst with their egg mass within their bodies. A female scale insect can lay more than 150 eggs in its reproductive phase.

The soft scales are known colloquially as 'cottony scales', 'cottony soft scales' or 'cushion bears'. These common names help to describe the cottony egg sacs (ovisacs) of adult female scales.

Some of the more serious scale-insect species affecting olive trees are as follows.

Family Coccidae

Soft scales

- Black scale *Saissetia oleae* (Olivier, 1791)
- Hemispherical scale *Saissetia coffeae* (Walker, 1852)
- Brown soft scale *Coccus hesperidum* (Linnaeu, 1758)
- Viburnum scale / Cushion scale *Lichtensia viburni* (Signoret, 1873)
- Carinated cottony scale *Filippia follicularis* (Targ, 1867) = *Fillipia oleae* (Costa, 1857)
- *Metaceronema japonica* (Maskell, 1897)

Family Diaspididae

Armoured (hard) scales

- Oleander scale *Aspidiotus nerii* (Bouché, 1833)
- Violet scale *Parlatoria oleae* (Colvée, 1880)
- *Lepidosaphes destefanii* (Leonardi, 1907) = *L. flava* (Signoret, 1870)
- Oystershell scale / Mussel scale *Lepidosaphes ulmi* (Linnaeus, 1758)
- Red scale *Aonidiella aurantii* (Maskell, 1879)
- Greedy scale *Hemiberlesia rapax* (Comstock, 1881)

- *Leucaspis riccae* (Targ, 1881)
- *Pseudaulacaspis pentagona* (Targ, 1886)
- San Jose scale *Quadraspidiotus perniciosus* (Com, 1881), *Q. lenticularis* (Lind, 1912), *Q. maleti* (Bal, 1950) = *Diaspidiotus maleti* (Vays, 1920)
- *Melanaspis corticosa* (Brain, 1919)
- Ross scale (Araucaria black scale; Round black scale) *Lindingaspis rossi* (Maskell, 1892)
- Circular black scale *Chrysomphalus aonidum* (Linnaeus, 1758)
- Latania scale *Hemiberlesia lataniae* (Signoret, 1869)

Family Asterolecaniidae

Pit scale

- *Pollinia pollini* (Costa, 1857)

Family Ortheziidae

Ensign scale

- *Orthezia olivicola* (Beingolea, 1965) = *Praelongorthezia olivicola* (Kozar, 2004)

Some of the more serious scale-insect species affecting olive trees are as follows:

Black scale

Sanssetia oleae (Olivier, 1791)

One of the most economically significant olive pests globally. Sap suction reduces plant vigour, however the main damage is caused by a decrease in photosynthesis due the appearance of sooty mould caused by fungus in the genus *Capnodium*.

Geographical distribution: Widely distributed.

Damage: Leaves, twigs, branches, trunks and fruits. Heavy infestations on leaves and branches cause extensive dieback and reductions in yield. In the case of table olives it detracts from the value of the product, while for oil olives it lowers the quality and quantity of the oil produced.

Economic importance: Causes serious economic damage.

Scale insects are sap-sucking with a lifecycle of incomplete metamorphosis and immature stages known as 'crawlers' and nymphs.

Females of some species lay eggs, while others, such as female red scales, give birth to live crawlers, which disperse to find a place to feed.

Most soft scales often have only one or two generations per year, while most armoured scales can have several. Eggs of both types of scales are usually hidden under the mother's cover and are not visible. Eggs hatch into tiny, usually yellow crawlers with legs. The adult female dies soon after the eggs have hatched. Eggs hatch beneath the female scale covering and the first instars migrate to new growth and immediately settle and insert their mouthparts. The first instar is called a crawler, because it possesses legs and is the only motile stage, with the exception of winged adult males. The crawler stage may be dispersed by wind or rain, or carried on the bodies of birds, other insects, or mammals. Crawler dispersal is usually limited to short distances.

Young black scales excrete sticky, shiny honeydew on leaves and fruits of infested trees. At first, affected trees and leaves glisten and then become sooty and black in appearance as sooty mould fungus grows on the honeydew. This situation restricts photosynthesis by the olive tree and causes weakening.

Controlling the scale will also get rid of the sooty mould.

Armoured scales do not produce honeydew. Heavy infestations seriously deform fruit, and fruit spotting renders the olive worthless.

Honeydew is a sugar-rich sticky liquid, secreted by aphids, mealybugs and some scale insects as they feed on plant sap. A black fungus known as sooty mould grows on the honeydew and its presence reduces photosynthesis and discolours affected fruit. Honeydew is used as a food source by ants (see section on Ants), which actively transport the insects (aphids, mealybugs and scales) and position them on the plant. As aphids, mealybugs and scales congregate in hidden places, or on the lower leaf surface, they may initially not be obvious.

Black scale.

Adults and nymphs of black scale, *Saissetia oleae*.

Saissetia coffeaea scale. (AGRICULTURA TACNA)

Brown soft scale, *Coccus hesperidum.* (NATURALIST)

Violet scale, *Parlatoria oleae*, on fruits and leaves in Turkey. (AZIZ OZKAN)

Viburnum cushion scale, *Lichtensia viburni,* on leaves.

Viburnum cushion scale eggs and nymphs. (NATURAMEDITERRANEO)

Red scale, *Aonidiella aurantii*, on fruits and leaves.

Oleander scale, *Aspidiotus nerii*. (D. Perdikis, Agricultural University of Athens, Greece)

Armoured black scale, *Chrysomphalus aonidum*, on olive fruits and leaf.

Oystershell scale, *Lepidosaphes ulmi*, adults and first-stage crawlers. (Whitney Cranshaw, University Bugwood.org)

Aggregation pattern of *Melanaspis corticosa* scale on an infested branch. (G. Mazzeo, University of Catania, Italy)

Colonies of pit scale, *Pollinia pollini* – fixed on buds and an enlarged view of a colony. This species is a serious pest of olive trees. (D. Houas, Le Kef University of Jendouba, Tunisia)

Ensign scale

Orthezia olivicola (Beingolea, 1965)
= *Praelongorthezia olivicola* [Hemiptera: Ortheziidae]

Geographical distribution: South America.
Damage: Twigs and leaves.
Morphology: This is one of the most difficult pests to control in olive groves in southern Peru. Adult ensign scales have six dark-coloured legs, a pair of dark antennae and stalked eyes. The apexes of the antennae have thick terminal bristly setae. There are several abdominal spiracles and an anal ring on the dermal surface, with pores and setae. The upper surface of the body is covered in a thick waxy secretion giving it a decorated, fluted appearance. It uses many host plants, including olives. Initially, outbreaks are detected in the orchards, but later the insects disperse, thanks to their great mobility.
Economic importance: A pest of potential economic importance.

Orthezia olivicola scale on leaves in Peru. (AGRICULTURA TACNA)

Mealybugs

Long-tailed mealybug *Pseudococcus longispinus* (Targ-Toz, 1867)

- Obscure mealybug *Pseudococcus viburni* (Signoret, 1875)
- Cotton mealybug / Solanim mealybug *Phenacoccus solani* (Ferris, 1918)
- Mango mealybug *Drosicha mangiferae* (Steb, 1903)

Geographical distribution: South America and Mediterranean Region.
Damage: Leaves.
Economic importance: Occasional pest on olives.

Long-tailed mealybug on leaves. (NATUREOFHOME)

Long-tailed mealybug on leaves.

Aphids

Prociphilus oleae (Leach, 1826) [Hemiptera: Aphididae]

Geographical distribution: Croatia, France, Greece, Italy, Spain and Turkey.
Damage: Leaves, shoots and trunks.
Morphology: Winged adult 4mm (0.16in) long, with yellow-brown abdomen.
Larval colonies covered with cottony wax, situated near base of olive twig. Occurs on suckers, mostly in shady areas towards base of trunk. Usually only one colony per shoot, but exceptionally up to five per shoot in Greece.
This is the only aphid species that infests olive trees. It is a rather rare aphid, with infestations only occuring in years and in environments that are particularly favourable to its development.
Economic importance: An occasional minor pest of olives.

Larval colony of *Prociphilus oleae* cottony wax near the base of an olive twig.

Stink bugs and allies

Brown marmorated stink bug (BMSB)

Halyomorpha halys (Stål, 1855) [Hemiptera: Pentatomidae]

Geographical distribution: East Asia (native), but began to spread to North America and Europe in 1998.
Damage: Fruit.
Morphology: Adult 12–17mm (0.47–0.67in) long. Has a mottled grey-brown shield-shaped body with distinctive stripes on the head and dark antennae, each with three or four pale stripes. A mass of 20–30 eggs are attached side-by-side on the underside of the host plant's leaves. Nymphs are yellow and red, and as they grow the yellow fades to white. These bugs emit a pungent odour when disturbed. At different developmental stages the stink bugs puncture olive fruits. The damage produced by feeding activity largely exceeds the area of the puncture, also causing fruit necrosis. Such damage to olives can be severe and it may be associated with early drop.
Economic importance: A pest that causes serious economic damage.

Adult Brown marmorated stink bug.

Brown marmorated stink bug eggs with first-stage nymphs. (MICHELE DELL'ORO)

Brown marmorated stink bug – different nymph stages. (MICHELE DELL'ORO)

Green vegetable bug / Green stink bug / Green shield bug / Southern green stink bug

Nezara viridula (Linnaeus, 1758) [Hemiptera: Pentatomidae]

Geographical distribution: Widely distributed.

Damage: Fruit.

Morphology: Adult shield-shaped, about 15mm (0.6in) long, and usually green; overwintering adults are brownish-purple. Female lays 30–130 eggs at a time, in the form of an egg mass glued firmly to the bottom of a leaf. The eggs are barrel-shaped, with an opening on the top. There are

Adult *Nezara viridula.*

Eggs of *Nezara viridula.*

Nezara viridula eggs with first-stage nymphs.

Different nymph stages of *Nezara viridula.*

five nymphal stages; nymphs are brightly coloured orange, red, black and green. Considered the most important 'sucking bug' pest. Feeds on a wide range of plants including field crops, vegetables and garden plants. It appears to visit olives from other plants or crops, attacking mainly table-olive fruit, increasing fruit rots such as anthracnose, but also causing direct sucking damage. It generally pierces the fruiting parts of plants and sucks out the juices.
Economic importance: Causes serious economic damage.

Damage to olive fruits by *Nezara viridula.*

Green stink bug

Plautia affinis (Dallas, 1851) [Hemiptera: Pentatomidae]

Very similar to the previous species, but smaller and with a brown pattern on the elytra.

Green stink bug damage to olive fruits in Egypt. (M. EL-KHOLY)

Green stink bug, Plautia affinis. (BRISBANEINSECT)

Leaf-footed bug

Leptoglossus phyllopus (Linnaeus, 1767) [Hemiptera: Coreidae]

Geographical distribution: Florida (USA).
Damage: Fruits.
Morphology: Adult 16–20mm (0.63–0.79in) long; male smaller than female. Sucks juices from plants by puncturing them with the mouthparts. A toxin is injected into the plant when piercing its skin, causing discolouration and hard spots on fruits. The adult bugs are highly resistant to pesticides; however, they are vulnerable in their bright orange nymph stage. Trap crops can be used to lure them away from desired plants and to encourage predator populations. They are able to fly, making a buzzing noise when airborne.
Economic importance: Occasional pest for olives in Florida.

Leaf-footed bug, *Leptoglossus phyllopus*, on an olive tree in Florida. (SANDRA A. ALLAN, USDA-ARS-CMAVE)

Olive psyllid

Euphyllura olivina (Costa, 1839) and *E. pakistanica* (Loginova, 1973) and *E. phillyreae* (F.) [Hemiptera: Psyllidae]

Geographical distribution: Mediterranean Region through Middle East to India.
Damage: Leaves, buds, young shoots, stems, inflorescences and fruiting shoots.
Morphology: Adults 2.4–2.8mm (0.09–0.11in) long and chubby, wings folded roof-like at rest. Pale green when young, later turning darker hazelnut-green when older. Eggs are inserted mostly on the inner surface of the young small leaves of apical buds. The five larval instars are flattened and ochre to pale yellow. The larvae produce a white waxy secretion and spherical honeydew droplets covering the infested buds, inflorescences and other tender growth they feed on.

Euphyllura olivina. (TAEBWD)

Euphyllura olivina. (MANUEL RUIZ TORRES)

Euphyllura olivina appears in the form of cotton-like masses, inside which the pest takes refuge on olive flowers, and its damage to trees is to reduce the percentage of flowering. (ADMINFARMERSNETLY)

Using their mouthparts to pierce and suck, adults and larvae feed on the sap they extract from leaf and flower buds, shoots, flowers, and young fruits. They overwinter as adults, sheltered on the underside of olive twigs and especially at the bases of leaves and buds.

Direct damage includes inflorescence abortion or withering and drop, leading to lower fruit set rates. Indirect damage sees plant debilitation due to the growth of sooty mould after larval secretions of honeydew.
Economic importance: Important pest of olives.

Olive whitefly

Aleurolobus olivinus (Silvestri, 1911) and *Siphoninus phillyreae* (Halliday, 1835) [Hemiptera: Aleyrodidae]

Geographical distribution: Widely distributed.
Damage: Leaves.
Morphology: Whiteflies, or snow flies, are tiny with a wingspan of less than 3mm (0.12in) and a body length of 1–2mm (0.04–0.08in). These sap-sucking insects are often found on the undersides of leaves. Adults are whitish, covered with a white powdery wax. Active in summer and autumn with one or two generations annually, with each female depositing 50–60 eggs on upper leaf surfaces. Nymphs (or larvae) are a flattened oval shape, and look more like a scale insect. Feeding on the leaves causes some damage but most injury to plants is due to the excreted honeydew that is colonised by sooty mould.

Whiteflies, *Aleurolobus olivinus.*

Whitefly adults on the back of a leaf.

Economic importance: A minor, occasional pest of olives.

Olive lace bug (OLB)

Froggattia olivinia (Froggatt, 1901) [Hemiptera: Tingidae]

Geographical distribution: Australia.
Damage: Leaves.
Morphology: Adult 3mm (0.12in) long, mottled dark brown and cream with transparent lace-like wings. Both adults and nymphs are sapsuckers. Eggs are deposited in or on the tissue of newly developing leaves, usually along the midribs. The adult secretes a brownish to black substance that hardens over the eggs, which secures them to the leaf. Nymphs are found clustered on the undersides of leaves out of direct sunlight, while adults are less clustered and fly short distances.

In climates with mild winters, lace bugs can overwinter as eggs, nymphs and adults on olive trees. Eggs survive on leaves, while adults survive under bark, leaf or mulch debris, or by using other cover for protection.

Eggs that have overwintered on the tree usually begin to hatch in late winter

Olive lace bug adults and nymphs feed on the undersides of olive leaves, causing pin-head sized yellow spotting on the upper surfaces of the leaves.

Damage to leaves by olive lace bug.

Olive lace bug adult on underside of an olive leaf. The adult secretes a brownish to black substance that hardens over the eggs.

or spring. There are five nymphal instars. Depending on the weather, the life cycle requires four to seven weeks, and there are one to four generations per year that can be completed before the final-generation adults lay overwintering eggs to complete the annual cycle.

Economic importance: A serious olive-tree pest in Australia, which can cause heavy defoliation and total crop failure if not managed effectively.

Olive tingit / Lace bug

Plerochila australis (Distant, 1904), *Eteoneus sigillatus* (Drake and Poor, 1936) and other species [Hemiptera: Tingidae]

Geographical distribution: South Africa and India.

Damage: Leaves.

Morphology: Grey-brown adult 4mm (0.16in) long. Feeds on the underside of olive leaves by sucking plant sap, destroying the leaf tissue. As a result, yellow spots appear on the leaf – in the case of heavy infestation the whole leaf turns yellow and dies.

Four closely related species of lace bugs can be found on olives in South Africa (*C. lineata*, *P. australis*, *Neoplerochila* sp., and *N. paliatseasi*), of which *P. australis* is the most frequent in olive groves.

Economic importance: These are pests of potential economic importance.

Rutherglen bug

Nysius vinitor (Bergroth, 1891) [Hemiptera: Lygaeidae]

Geographical distribution: Western Australia.
Damage: Young olive trees.
Morphology: Grey-brown adult 4mm (0.16in) long with clear wings folded flat on back. They have a narrow body with prominent dark eyes, sucking and piercing mouthparts, and are highly mobile. Nymphs are wingless and have a dark red, pear-shaped body. This sap-sucking insect generally lives in pasture and commonly breeds on weeds, but in drier areas such as in Western Australia it has attacked young olive trees leading to dieback. As trees mature and grow higher, the impact of these insects becomes insignificant.

Rutherglen bug, *Nysius vinitor*. (EDITHVALE)

Adults migrate in large numbers, often assisted by storms or strong winds.
Economic importance: A pest of potential economic importance.

Plant bug

Closterotomus trivialis (Costa,1853) [Hemiptera: Miridae]

Geographical distribution: Italy, Greece, Portugal and Spain.
Damage: Buds and flowers.
Morphology: Adult 6.6–7.9mm (0.26–0.31in) long. Body colour variable – female usually yellow and green with a yellow-green head. Has a single generation annually (it is univoltine) and overwinters in the egg stage in bark cracks. Females oviposit their eggs at the end of spring. Eggs hatch in late winter to early spring and the larvae feed on understorey weeds. This bug can cause serious fruit abortion.
Economic importance: A serious pest of olives in the Mediterranean Basin.

Plant bug, *Closterotomus trivialis*. (D. PERDIKIS, AGRICULTURAL UNIVERSITY OF ATHENS)

Barrillo

Agalmatium flavescens (Olivier, 1791) = *Hysteropterum grylloides* (Fabricius, 1794) [Hemiptera: Issidae]

Both images above: Barrillo, *Hysteropterum grylloides*, in Italy. (RA PISANO)

Geographical distribution: Mediterranean Region.
Damage: Leaves, fruits and young shoots.
Morphology: Adult 5–7mm (0.2–0.3in) long, brownish with light and dark spots. Lays eggs on bark of olive trees. In spring a multitude of small mud crusts attached to each other on the trunks and branches of the olive tree indicate the presence of the young insects – for this reason it is known by the common name of Barrillo, meaning 'pimple'. It does not produce direct perceptible damage, although it can cause floral abortions and injuries in young branches. The larvae suck the sap of leaves, fruits and young shoots of olives. To be considered a problem, it has to colonise much of the cortex.
Economic importance: A pest of potential economic importance.

Adult *Agalmatium flavescens*. (ILIA GJONOV)

Spittlebug

Philaenus spumarius (Linnaeus, 1758) [Hemiptera: Aphrophoridae]

Geographical distribution: Widely distributed.
Damage: Leaves and shoots.
Morphology: Adult 5–7mm (0.2–0.3in) long. In these polymorphic sap-sucking insects the body colour is very variable and about 20 different colours are known. The young insect protects itself from predators by creating a protective shield using bubbles from the sap it has extracted from the plant.

Spittlebugs are univoltine, overwintering as eggs and with a development cycle

Spittlebug adult. (STEVE SCHOLNICK)

Spittlebug nymph, *Philaenus spumarius.* (JOE BULLOCK)

consisting of five instars before the emergence of the adults. The movement of nymphs is limited, and under current epidemiological scenarios in European outbreaks, these do not contribute to the spread of infection. Adults can acquire and transmit bacterium soon after feeding on infected plants (without a latency period) and throughout their whole lifespan, thereby challenging the effectiveness of chemical control to protect plants from infections during the whole adult season.

Economic importance: Spittlebugs are vectors of the bacterium *Xylella fastidiosa* in Europe – the causal agent of olive dieback. Therefore they are a pest of potential economic importance.

Glassy-winged sharpshooter

Homalodisca vitripennis (Germar, 1821) [Hemiptera: Cicadellidae]

Geographical distribution: USA.

Damage: Stems, trunks, branches and leaf petioles.

Morphology: Adult about 13mm (0.5in) long, with a large flat head and prominent eyes. Female lays up to 28 eggs in a cluster on the underside of young fully developed leaves and dusts the egg mass with a secretion that resembles white chalk. Nymphs hatch in 10–14 days and progress through five growth stages before reaching adulthood. The adult lifespan is approximately two months. There are usually two complete generations per year with adults hibernating in forest areas over winter.

Economic importance: In isolation the sharpshooter does not cause significant damage to host plants. However, infestations can be fatal when the insect acts as a vector for the bacterium *Xylella fastidiosa*, which is the cause of olive dieback.

Glassy-winged sharpshooter.

Cicadas [Hemiptera: Cicadidae]

Black prince cicada, *Psaltoda plaga*.

Redeye cicada, *Psaltoda moerens*.

Cicada damage on a twig.

Cicada eggs in stem. (JOE BOGGS, OSU EXTENSION)

Species associated with olives include:

- Redeye cicada *Psaltoda moerens* (Germar, 1834)
- Silver knight cicada / Black prince cicada *Psaltoda plaga* (Walker, 1850)
- *Cicada orni* (Linnaeus, 1758)
- *Lyristes plebejus* (Scopoli, 1763)
- *Tibicen plebejus* (Scopoli, 1763)
- *Cicadetta brullei* (Fieber, 1876)
- *Psalmocharias plagifera* (Schum, 1922)

Geographical distribution: Widely distributed.

Damage: Young trees and twigs.

Morphology: Adult 20–50mm (1–2in) long in most species. Cicadas have stout bodies with two pairs of wings and prominent compound eyes set wide apart on the sides of the head. They also have three small ocelli located on the top of the head in a triangle between the two large eyes; this distinguishes cicadas from other members of the Hemiptera. The cicada life cycle has three stages: egg, nymph and adult. Cicada nymphs use their sucking mouthparts to drink sap from the xylem of various tree species, sometimes causing damage to trees,

mainly in the form of scarring left on tree branches where the females laid their eggs. Branches of young trees may die as a result.
Economic importance: Cicadas are not major horticultural pests but in some outbreak years they could be considered a potential pest on olives in Turkey, Italy and Tunisia (south-west region).

Cicada exoskeletons on a tree trunk after the insect has emerged.

Evidence of cicadas feeding. To feed, the adults sink their stylus into branches and extract the sap, causing an oily stain with a white centre. (NICOLO PETRIGNANO)

Order Orthoptera: Grasshoppers and Crickets

Katydids or bush crickets

Scudderia sp. [Orthoptera: Tettigoniidae]

Geographical distribution: Florida (USA).
Damage: Leaves.
Morphology: Adult 36–50mm (1.4–2in). Also known as 'long-horned grasshoppers', although they are more closely related to crickets. Katydids have long antennae and sword-like ovipositors, while grasshoppers have short antennae and blunt ovipositors. Another difference is in their egg-laying

Katydid (*Scudderia* sp.). (WIKIPEDIA)

behaviour – katydids lay their eggs on plant parts while grasshoppers lay theirs on the ground. Eggs are deposited in olive leaves between the upper and lower leaf surfaces, along the leaf margin. Growers have reported minor chewing and defoliation damage from grasshoppers and katydids on olive trees in Florida.

Economic importance: An occasional pest for olives.

Wingless grasshopper and Locust [Orthoptera: Acrididae]

Phaulacridium vittatum and *Chortoicetes terminifera*

These two species are significant agricultural pests in Australia. In the non-swarming phase, the grasshoppers feed primarily on terminal leaf margins. The wingless grasshopper is an occasional pest for olives in Western Australia. The locust devours most green plant material, but no damage has been found on olives.

Wingless grasshopper, *Phaulacridium vittatum*, in Western Australia. (DAFWA)

Grasshoppers hiding in the cracks of an olive tree trunk.

Order Hymenoptera: Wasps and Ants

Olive seed wasps

Eupelmus spermophilus (Silvestri, 1915) [Hymenoptera: Chalcidoidea]

Geographical distribution: South Africa (Western Cape).

Damage: Fruits.

Morphology: Commonly found in cultivated and wild olives. Females lay eggs early in the season when the inside of the olive seed is soft – this allows the larvae to feed on the kernel and pupate. Adult wasps emerge from olives by chewing a hole through the pit and flesh, leaving characteristic emergence holes.

Economic importance: Does not pose

a significant threat to the olive industry and cannot be considered a key pest of olives. However, during some seasons it can affect yields as it causes premature fruit drop; this usually happens when wild olive trees are located close to commercial olive groves.

Ants [Hymenoptera: Formicidae]

Geographical distribution: Widely distributed.
Damage: The ants disrupt biological control of scale insects.
Morphology: Adults 2–12mm (0.08–0.48in) long.
High levels of ant activity on olive trees often indicate significant populations of honeydew- producing insects such as scale insects. Ants do not cause any direct damage to olives, but they disrupt the biological control of black scale.

Ants are attracted to honeydew excreted by scale insects. (HOUZZ)

Ants enter the tree canopy searching for honeydew secreted by the scale insects and they interfere with scale predators and parasites, thereby favouring the development of black scale infestations. The movement of ants up a trunk is indicative of active black scale in the tree, even if the scale insects are not immediately obvious. Ant activity can therefore be a useful indicator of which trees to check more closely for this pest. An exception is that ant activity may be high during flowering time, when the ants are attracted to nectar. Management of black scale will reduce ant problems, and vice-versa.

Leaf-cutting ants [Hymenoptera: Formicidae]

- *Acromyrmex crassispinus* (Forel)
- *Acromyrmex laticeps* (Emery)
- *Acromyrmex lundii* (Guérin)
- *Acromyrmex striatus* (Roger)
- *Acromyrmex ambiguus* (Emery)

Geographical distribution: Brazil.
Damage: Leaves.
Morphology: Seven species of these ants have been found both in seedlings and in adult olive trees. They can cause severe damage in some plants, leading to the death of some specimens. The leaf-cutting ant species listed above have been found in olive groves in Rio Grande do Sul state.

Order Blattodea: Termites

Termites [Blattodea: Termitoidae]

Geographical distribution: South Africa, India, Australia and Mediterranean Region.

Damage: In drier regions termites can damage young trees by nesting in the root systems. In South Africa they also feed on twigs and leaves.

Morphology: Termites are usually small or medium sized, whitish or colourless insects, with short antennae. They have strong biting mouthparts with which to chew seeds, wood or leaves.

Economic importance: An occasional pest for olives.

Termite mound next to olive tree.

Other Pests

Order Acarina: Mites

Eriophyd mites (Acarina: Eriophyidae)

Geographical distribution: Widely distributed.
Damage: Buds, flowers, leaves and fruits.
Morphology: Olive orchards are home to several species of plant-eating mites belonging to different families. Eriophyid mites include species of blister, bud, gall and rust mites, which are named after the deformities that they cause. The mites are very small, cigar-shaped and translucent yellow, pink or white, with two sets of front legs located by the head.

Species range between 0.1–0.3mm (less than 0.01in) in length and can only be seen with the aid of a hand lens with a magnification of 20x or greater. Plant quality is reduced by feeding damage, which can lead to deformities, such as galls, erinea (felty areas of dense leaf hairs), brooms (deformed masses of twigs or branches), leaf blistering, curling, rusts and silvering. The mites disperse by travelling on the wind or riding on insects, birds or clothing. They seek microenvironments under bud scales, in growing points or at the petiole base of leaves.

Three of the key mite species found on olive trees are as follows:

Olive gall mite *Aceria oleae* (Nalepa, 1900)

By feeding within the growing points of the olive, the mite causes the emerging leaves to be deformed and twisted, as well as bulges or knobs on the fruits. Attacks on flowers and fruits result in drying and flower drop, premature dropping of fruits, or fruit malformations. Mature fruits are not attacked. Prefers young olives growing in warm and humid conditions, thus thriving in nurseries and well-irrigated young plantations, and infesting mainly the peripheral growth. Passes the winter hidden on the lower sides of leaves, with populations moving to flower clusters in spring.

Olive bud mite *Oxycenus maxwelli* (Keifer, 1939)

Heavy infestations can cause the premature fall of olive flowers, as well as spotting and distortion of leaves. Most severe in young trees, causing shortened internodes, malformation of shoots and curling of leaves.

Aceria oleae attacking leaves. (AGRIO)

Oxycenus maxwelli feeding on an olive leaf.

Olive rust mite *Tegolophus hassani* (Keifer, 1959)

Causes russeting and deformation on the leaves that reduces the quantity and quality of olives. During heavy infestations, mites twist and deform leaves, cause misshaped fruits and seriously reducing the amount and quality of olives available for picking.

In addition to the above three species, to date seven other mite species are known to be eriophyids on olives. These are:

- *Aceria olivi* (Zaher and Abou-Awad)
- *Aculops benakii* (Hatzinikolis)
- *Aculus olearius* (Castagnoli)
- *Ditrymacus athiasellus* (Keifer)
- *Oxycenus niloticus* (Zaher and Abou-Awad)
- *Shevtchenkella barensis* (Vidovic and Petanovic)
- *Tegonotus oleae* (Natcheff)

Economic importance: Pests of potential economic importance.

Order Nematoda: Nematodes

Nematodes

- **Root-decay nematode** *Tylenchulus semipenetrans* Cobb
- **Root-knot nematodes** *Meloidogyne arenaria* (Neal) Chitwood, *M. hapla* Chitwood, *M. incognita* (Kofoid and White) Chitwood, *M. javanica* (Treub) Chitwood
- **Root-lesion nematodes** *Pratylenchus penetrans* (Cobb) Sher and Allen and *P. vulnus* Allen and Jensen
- **Root-necrosis nematodes / Spiral nematodes** *Helicotylenchus* sp. and *Rotylenchus* sp.
- **Grazer nematodes** *Tylenchus* spp.

- **Stunt nematodes** *Tylenchorhynchus* spp. Plant-parasitic nematodes are major damaging pests on olive trees, mainly in nurseries. Symptoms vary from unthriftiness to stunting and leaf yellowing. They damage plants by directly attacking roots and subsequently predisposing them to secondary infections by bacteria and fungi, causing olive preplant problems. Parasitic nematodes spread with movement of soil, water and infected plants.

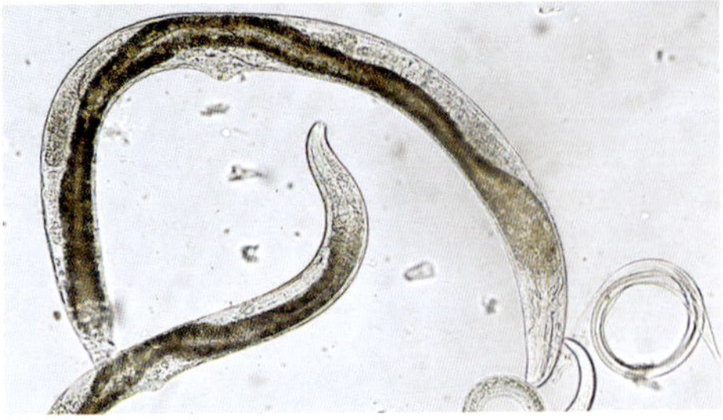

Nematodes.

Root-knot nematodes cause the formation of galls or knots on the roots.

Order Mollusca: Snails

Snails (Mollusca: Gastropoda)

Snail species associated with olives include:

- Brown snail (*Microxeromagna vestita*)
- Italian snail (*Theba pisana*)
- Conical snail (*Prietocella barbara*)

ALL IMAGES: Snails rest on olive trees, smothering trunks, branches and leaves.

Snails can infest olive trees causing stress through defoliation and reduced photosynthesis, smothering trunks and branches, and occasionally causing broken limbs from their weight.

Moisture, either from heavy dews or rainfall, will trigger snails to become active and descend to the soil surface. Generally found in alkaline sandy soils high in calcium. Adults lay egg masses in moist soil. Eggs hatch in two to four weeks.

Vertebrate Pests

Birds

Growers in some areas report birds eating and damaging olive fruits at harvest or while on trees, with a strong preference for particular cultivars.

Birds can cause considerable damage by snapping off branches, especially in young trees. In Australia, for example, cockatoos, including corellas and galahs, appear to be the main culprits. While birds often get a bad reputation for snacking on fruit, insectivorous birds are excellent pest controllers.

Bird damage to olive fruit.

Rabbits and Hares

Including *Oryctolagus cuniculus*, *Lepus capensis* and others

Rabbits and hares chew the bark on trunks, weakening the olive trees. Young planted trees need to be protected against attack with protective sleeves. These animals not only ring-bark young trees, but can damage olive trees up to 10 or 15 years old.

Rabbit burrow and olive tree bark damage caused by rabbits.

Wombats

Wombat burrow under an olive tree.

There are three species of wombats, which are exclusively Australian marsupials:

- **Common Wombat** *Vombatus ursinus*
- **Northern Hairy-nosed Wombat** *Lasiorhinus krefftii*
- **Southern Hairy-nosed Wombat** *Lasiorhinus latifrons*

These ground-dwelling animals don't generally damage trees but have been known to dig burrows under or near olive trees. Up to 20m (65ft) long with numerous connecting tunnels and entrances, the burrows can cause problems for heavy vehicles in the orchard.

Feral pig *Sus scrofa*

Widespread environmental and agricultural pests. Evidence of wild pigs is obvious even if you don't see the animals physically. The pigs use their snouts to root up the ground in search of food, including plant roots and other items.

Control: Fencing can be extremely effective but the cost is often prohibitive. Trapping can be an effective method of removing wild pigs from an olive grove.

Feral pig damage in an olive grove. (PATRICE NEWEL)

Voles

Rodents belonging to the genera *Microtus* and *Pitymys* may cause damage to olive orchards in Europe. They live underground and dig an extensive network of tunnels, feeding on roots, bulbs and rhizomes. Because the roots are affected, the tree can become debilitated. Damage can be very serious in young orchards and this can even cause the death of some trees.

Kangaroos and Wallabies

These Australian marsupials sometimes cause damage to olive trees. During times of drought, when there is a shortage of grass, wallabies eat leaves and twigs from olive trees and can kill young trees. Kangaroos also cause occasional damage to trees, although generally this is not as severe as that from wallabies.

Kangaroo in an olive grove.

Wallaby eating olive leaves.

Sheep

Some olive growers let sheep graze on the orchard floor to control weeds, however they can cause severe damage to olive trees by eating bark and chewing foliage when their normal diet of grass runs out.

Damage to bark on olive tree caused by sheep.

Horses, Deer, Goats and Cattle

Horses have been known to devour young olive trees. Deer, goats and cattle can break branches and eat lower foliage. Cattle in particular are known to cause damage by rubbing themselves against trees. Deer can also cause olive trees quite severe damage by breaking branches when trying to rub off their seasonal antlers; this can enable insects, rain or frost to cause further damage to the tree.

Goat eating olive leaves and twigs.

CHAPTER 2

Diseases

Fungal Diseases

Olive trees can be attacked by different fungal pathogens. These attack different tree parts, including the roots, stem, leaves, flowers and fruits. Some of them obligate parasites and others are primary or secondary invaders, known as saprophytes. Many scientists consider some species as saprophytes and parasites at the same times, depending to several conditions such as temperature, sensitivity of the host and viability of the species.

- Saprogenesis is the part of the pathogen's life cycle when it is not in vital association with living host tissue and either continues to grow in dead host tissue or becomes dormant.
- Many of the most common phytopathogens are usually present and asymptomatic in olive growing, and the most frequent infections depend mainly on favourable climatic conditions and by inadequate agronomic practices.

Environmental factors affecting disease development

Important environmental factors that may affect the development of plant diseases and determine whether they become epiphytotic include temperature, relative humidity, soil moisture, soil pH, soil type and soil fertility.

Diseases of olive fruits can cause financial losses through the direct loss of rotted fruits, the reduced cosmetic value of table olives, and the reduced quality of the oil due to fungal infections. Major fungal diseases affecting the olive-tree canopy that are associated with fruit rot in olive-growing countries include Anthracnose, Cercosporiose, Peacock Spot and Dalmatian Disease.

Foliar and Fruit Diseases

Anthracnose

Several species of *Colletotrichum* have been indicated as responsible for olive anthracnose in different countries, including: *Colletotrichum acutatum* (J. H. Simmonds), *C. gloeosporioides* ((Penz.) Penz. and Sacc.), *C. simmondsii, C. clavatum, C. alienum,*

C. boninense, C. fioriniae, C. fructicola C. theobromicola, C. nymphaeae, C. godetiae, C. perseae, C. aenigma, C. siamense, C. karsti, C. queenslandicum, C. cigarro.

Geographical distribution: Anthracnose is a major disease of olives in many olive-growing countries worldwide.

Damage: Flower buds, flowers, sepals, pedicels, peduncles, leaves, stems, fruit set, immature fruit, ripe fruit, receptacles, petioles, green shoots, twigs, suckers and waterspouts; fungal conidia on the bark of olive trees.

Symptoms: The disease may cause blossom blight, mummified fruits and premature fruit drop, while major fruit losses occur during ripening. What distinguishes the disease is the pink/orange colour on the surface of rotting fruits. It also causes leaf necrosis, branch dieback and defoliation and death of woody organs.

Brown lesions with anthracnose fungal spores observed in young green stems and leaves, and dieback of young shoot tips in early spring and summer.

Also, flowering or fruit set and immature fruits can be observed during fruit development on a single peduncle (both flowers and fruit set late in the season, in summer rather than spring, and carry fungal infection).

Anthracnose causes soft, circular rots on fruit close to harvest time. The spores live on in infected, mummified fruit. This is another reason why it is important to harvest the entire crop and rake up and bin any windfall.

Latent infections: Susceptibility to anthracnose begins in early stages during flower development and increases during blossoming. Different olive cultivars have varying responses to flower infection. Infection of flower buds and flowers by anthracnose is mostly symptomless. During this symptomless biotrophic phase, the pathogen invades the host without killing it and feeds on living cells. Re-infection of the tree by the repeating conidial stage is then responsible for increased anthracnose symptoms during summer, leading to new growth suckers, waterspouts and fruits.

Immature olive fruits are susceptible to disease at all physiological stages of growth. The infection remains latent until the fruits begin to ripen. The ability to survive and multiply in the absence of symptoms may explain why anthracnose fungi often cause unexpected crop losses in olives.

What distinguishes this disease is the rotting and mummification of unripe and ripe fruits of susceptible varieties. The infected fruit will rot and sometimes shrivel before prematurely dropping from the tree.

Hemibiotrophic anthracnose fungal pathogens grow first on living tissue and then cause host death in later, necrotrophic growth (*Colletotrichum* species – a parasitic organism that kills the living cells of its host and then feeds on the dead matter).

Transmission: Anthracnose fungal spores are spread by insects, moist wind, dew and water.

Several modes of penetration are possible: through natural openings such as stomata, through wounds, and by the direct penetration of the cuticle. Of these, direct penetration is the most common means of tissue penetration.

Olive fruit fly (*Bactrocera oleae*), Queensland fruit fly (*Bactrocera tryoni*) and green vegetable bug (*Nazara viridula*) can increase anthracnose severity by carrying fungal conidia, and provide entry points for fungal rots. Infection is spread by fungus from adjacent diseased fruit.

Weather conditions are very important for disease development: in particular, high rainfall or irrigation combined with summer heat can create a steamy, warm environment conducive to fungal growth. Warm, rainy, misty and humid conditions or heavy dews are associated with severe anthracnose epidemics.

Under favourable conditions, they produce creamy and orange slimy masses of spores on soft circular rots or sunken spots on the fruit. As humidity drops and the temperature increases, the affected olive fruits mummify and may remain on the tree, providing inoculum for new infections in summer.

The closer the fruits are to maturity, the greater their susceptibility to infection.

The *Colletotrichum* species then colonise the peduncle of affected fruits, which fall to the ground. However, after harvest some mummified fruits may remain in the tree canopy until the next autumn or winter. *Colletotrichum* fungi overwinter in mummified fruits on the tree, woody tissue and leaves; the fungus has long saprophytic survival ability on dead peduncles and pedicels.

The infection can persist from season to season, depending on the olive cultivar, environment, crop management and pathogen virulence; with fungal inoculum present year-round throughout the canopy. When pathogens are present on susceptible cultivars in conductive environmental conditions an epidemic can occur.

Economic importance: Anthracnose is one of the most serious olive fungal diseases in the world. The main disease of olive fruits causes serious economic damage and reduces plant productivity and the quality of olive oil. Anthracnose is also problematic for table olives because of its impact on taste and appearance.

The asymptomatic infection of flower buds and flowers. Different olive cultivars have varying responses to flower infection.

Anthracnose infection of flowers.

Flowering and fruit set carry fungal infection during fruit development and on a single peduncle.

Fruit set later in the season can carry fungal infection.

Fungus spreads from adjacent diseased fruits as contact infection.

Latent infection on fruit on the cultivar 'Barnea'. Affected fruits show necrotic lesions as immature fruits or at an early ripening stage, which progress until total fruit rot.

On affected fruits, the fungus develops asexual fruiting bodies (acervuli) that produce a mass of conidia in a pinkish-orange gelatinous matrix.

Fruit rot.

Anthracnose fungal spores on sepals and receptacles permit the survival of the pathogen during hot and dry summers.

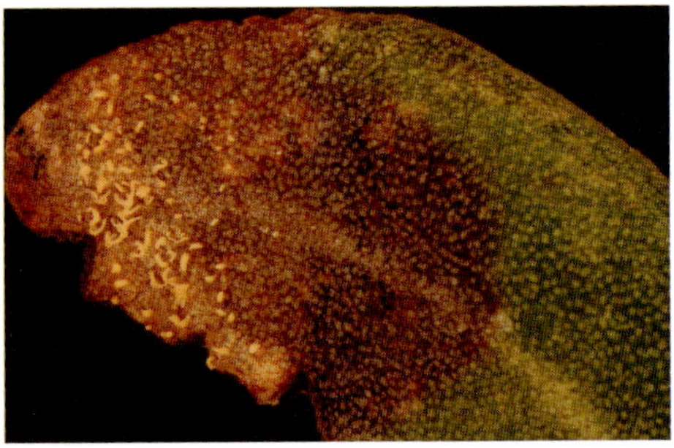

Apical leaves show necrotic margins, with fungal spores of anthracnose disease.

Young shoot infected by anthracnose fungus.

Shoot dieback.

Fungus infecting suckers.

Fungus infecting suckers.

Both images: Anthracnose fungi overwinter in mummified fruits on the tree, woody tissue and leaves.

Mummified fruits before harvest.

Symptoms of anthracnose after fungicide applications.

Cercosporiose, Cercospora leaf spot

Pseudocercospora cladosporioides (Sacc) U.Braun (syn. *Mycocentrospora cladosporioides* (Sacc) P.Costa ex Deigh)

Geographical distribution: Worldwide.
Damage: Leaves, fruits, twigs.
Symptoms: Cercosporiose is a serious disease a caused by the fungus *Pseudocercospora cladosporioides*. Cercospora olive leaf spot is particularly important since it causes leaf drop and partial defoliation of branches, which weakens the trees, reduces shoot growth and causes branch dieback and decreased fruit set. Cercosporiosis attacks on olive drupes in young and intensive groves have also been recorded.
Leaves: The first signs of disease are grey blotches on the undersides of the leaves, which appear to be covered with black dust or black sooty mould-like symptoms, even on green leaves without any lesions. Symptoms on upper leaf surfaces are initially slightly chlorotic areas (although some varieties show more chlorosis than others), which later develop into brown spots. Infected leaves fall, causing partial defoliation in some cases.

Fruits: Disease symptoms on the fruits can vary according to cultivar and fruit-ripening stage. Green olives develop irregular, slightly sunken dark brown spots. On ripening diseased fruit these brown spots appear with or without a halo (of pale brown or green to pale yellow discolouration, in sharp contrast to the fruit colour, surrounding the infected sites), with ash-grey appearance of fungal mycelium.

Diseased spots may enlarge and coalesce, covering a large portion of the fruit surface and reducing the crop.
Transmission: The pathogen is most severe when moist weather conditions prevail. High temperatures restrict spore germination and growth. Wind can also carry conidia from infected leaves. Outbreaks are sporadic, and the disease may

Disease symptoms on the fruits vary according to cultivar, ripening stage and locality.

Leaves showing high level of inoculum in spring.

Different types of symptoms on leaves.

Spore mass on olive leaves in late season.

take several years before it becomes serious enough in a particular locality to cause economic damage. Many infected leaves remain on the tree and act as a source of spores for later infections. Fungal inoculum present year-round throughout the canopy.

Economic importance: A serious defoliating disease, although fruit damage may be as important as leaf infection.

Peacock spot, olive scab, olive leaf spot, bird's-eye spot

Venturia oleaginea (Castagne) Rossman and Crous, *Cycloconium oleaginum* Castagne, *Spilocaea oleagina* (Hughes), *Fusicladium oleagineum* (Castagne) Ritschel and U. Braun

Geographical distribution: Worldwide.

Olive leaf spot, caused by *Venturia oleaginea*, is the most common fungal disease of olives.

Damage: Leaves, leaf petioles, fruit stems and fruits.

Symptoms: Peacock spot /olive leaf spot is a serious disease caused by the fungus. The disease can cause leaf-drop, occasionally to the point of complete defoliation. High levels of infection were observed on leaves before flowering, which resulted in flower drop and poor fruit set. Severe and recurrent attacks of the fungus provoke an intense defoliation and poor growth and dieback of defoliated branches.

Leaves: Typically causes round spots on the leaves, green-black in colour, often surrounded by a yellowish or red-purple halo. The halo is usually absent in autumn-winter, while in spring it is very noticeable both on young and older lesions. The dark colour of the spots is due to the spores of the causal agent, which can cover the entire spot or develop in concentric ring patterns.

On the underside of leaves, the symptoms are blackish areas along the central vein. Sometimes the lesion is limited only to the petiole of the leaf, which falls when it is still green or once it has turned yellow. At other times the lesion can affect the fruit peduncle, causing the olive to shrivel and drop early, together with the peduncle.

Latent infections: Old infections on leaves become crusty and whitish following high temperatures. In very hot or very cold conditions, the latent period was estimated to last for several weeks or even several

Peacock spot (white spots) on olive leaves and fruits. High temperatures restrict spore germination and growth, making the disease inactive during summer.

Peacock spot petioles.

Infection on leaves and fruit set.

Peacock spot on olive leaves.

Peacock spot on olive fruit.

Infection on veins of leaf.

Fruits infected by scab.

months. Because of this long latency period in the disease, initial infection is often missed before the characteristic spots appear.
Fruits: Fruit lesions on the affected parts remain green longer and have a pale brown hue or **grey spot** caused by the fungus. In severe attacks, the fungus grows and forms a true hard layer or **scab** on the surface of the olive.
Transmission: For favourable conditions for the spores to develop into an infection, moisture must remain on the leaves for several hours with mild temperatures. Usually the disease occurs sporadically, particularly in wet weather in spring and autumn. The disease is inactive during summer. While hot and dry weather discourages disease development, warm and humid weather during summer can encourage disease incidence.

The pathogen is generally known to survive as conidia in unfavourable conditions in dry, hot weather, in fallen leaves, and in infected leaves and fruits on the tree. Thus, peacock spot may be present all year round in olive groves if conditions are suitable.
Economic importance: Peacock spot is one of the most serious olive fungal diseases in the world, causing severe yield losses.

Dalmatian fruit rot

Botryosphaeria dothidea (Moug.) Cesati and De Notaris (= *Macrophoma dalmatica* (Thüm) Berl. and Voglino and *Sphaeropsis dalmatica* (Thüm.) Gigante = *Camarosporium dalmaticum* (Thüm.) Zachos andTzav.-Klon)

Botryosphaeria dothidea symptoms on fruit. (University of Cordoba)

Botryosphaeria dothidea symptoms on fruit.

Geographical distribution: Widespread in the Mediterranean basin.
Damage: Fruits.
Symptoms: Affects unripe fruit. The pathogen produces sunken, necrotic and elliptical or circular lesions, which are 8mm (0.3in) in diameter with sharp edges delineating infected and healthy tissues. Pseudothecia of *B. dothidea* occur on blighted olive shoots.

Transmission: The fungal spores invade the fruits through wounds caused by the olive fruit fly (*Bactrocera oleae*) and may even be transmitted by it. This fungus can infect fruit during the summer with high temperatures and low relative humidity. However, details of the influence of the environment and host are unclear.

Economic importance: Considered the most important disease of table fruit.

Lepra, Olive leprosy

Phlyctema vagabunda Desm. (syn: Neofabraea alba (E.J. Guthrie) Verkley *Neofabraea vagabunda* (Desm.) Rossman)

Lepra fruit rot caused by *Neofabraea vagabunda*. (UNIVERSITY OF CORDOBA)

Leaf lesion of *Neofabraea kienholzii*. (FLORENT TROUILLAS)

Geographical distribution: Spain, Portugal and California.

Damage: Fruits, leaves, shoots and twigs.

Symptoms: The fungi cause branch cankers and twig dieback as well as small, circular and necrotic lesions on leaves, and fruit rot.

Leprosy of olive trees affects the surface of olives, both green and ripe fruits. The symptoms of fruit leprosy consist of round, depressed necrotic lesions with a prominent darker edge that eventually causes the partial or full mummification of the fruit and its fall.

Transmission: Affected trees display numerous leaf and shoot lesions developing at wounds created by mechanical harvesters.

The 'Arbosana' cultivar was highly affected by the disease, whereas the disease was sporadic in 'Arbequina' and not found in 'Koroneiki'.

Other fruit rots

Geographical distribution: Worldwide. Other fungal species have also been found in olive fruit causing more or less significant diseases. Most fungal species causing fruit rot of olives are common saprophytes or secondary invaders normally penetrating through injuries made by biotic or abiotic factors. Wide arrays of fungal groups have been reported to cause fruit rot on olives including:

- *Alternaria alternata, A. infectoria, A. solani, A.* sp.
- *Arthrinium phaeospermum*
- *Aspergillus niger, A. ochraceus*
- *Aureobasidium pullulans*
- *Capnodium elaeophilum*
- *Cladosporium cladosporioides, C. herbarum*
- *Diplodia seriata*
- *Epicoccum nigrum*
- *Fusarium arthrosporioides/avenaceum, F. lateritium, F. moniliforme, F. nygamai, F. solani*
- *Neofusicoccum australe, N. luteum, N. mediterraneum, N. parvum, N. vitifusiforme*
- *Penicillium expansum, P.* spp.
- *Pestalotia fici*
- *Phomopsis* sp.
- *Pilidium concavum*
- *Rhizopus stolonifer*
- *Stemphylium amaranthi*
- *Trichoderma harzianum*
- *Trichothecium roseum*

Phytophtora fruit rot caused by *Phytophthora oleae* and *P. nicotianae* remained unnoticed for a long time as symptoms overlap or are confused with those of anthracnose in Italy and *Truncatella angustata* olive fruit rot resembling anthracnose disease symptoms recorded in Iran.

All the above fungi are capable of infecting olive fruit directly or indirectly, and reduce fruit yield significantly in heavily infected trees; besides, they can affect the commercial value of table olives and reduce the oil content and oil quality in oil-producing varieties.

Neofusicoccum luteum damage on olive fruits.

Trunk Diseases

Trunk Cankers, Branch and Twig Dieback, Leaf Necrosis

Trunk disease fungal pathogens reduce olive production globally by causing cankers and a general decline of trees, and they are often associated with dieback of twigs and branches. Dead or dying branches represent a reduced fruit-bearing capacity.

The symptoms comprise a general decline of the trees, beginning with foliar browning and leaf drop, wilting of apical shoots, dieback of twigs and branches, and brown streaking under the bark of the trunk, branches and twigs. There can also be discolouration, necrotic wood, and death of shoots. In advanced stages of the disease, necrosis and cankers are seen on the bark.

The fungal pathogens include:

- *Athelia rolfsii*
- *Arthrinium phaeospermum*
- *Biscogniauxia mediterranea, B. rosacearum*
- *Botryosphaeria dothidea, B. ribis,*
- *Cadophora luteo-olivacea,*
- *Celerioriella umnquma* sp. *nov.*
- *Coniothyrium ferrarisianum*
- *Coniochaeta fasciculata, C. velutina*
- *Cylindrocarpon destructans*
- *Cytospora oleina, C. oleicola, C. olivarum, C. plurivora, C. pruinosa, C. sorbicola*
- *Dactylonectria macrodidyma* and others
- *Diaporthe foeniculina, D. viticol*
- *Diatrype oregonensis, D. stigma*
- *Didymocyrtis banksiae*
- *Diplodia africana, D. fraxini, D. mutila, D. seriata, D. subglobosa*
- *Didymosphaeria variabile*
- *Dothiorella iberica, D. omnivora, D. sarmentorum, D. sempervirentis*
- *Eutypa lata*
- *Fomitiporella* sp.
- *Fusarium acuminatum, F. eumartii, F. lateritium, F. oxysporum, F. solani*
- *Heterotruncatella* sp.
- *Ilyonectria capensis, I. robusta*
- *Lasiodiplodia theobromae*
- *Neofabraea kienholzii*
- *Neofusicoccum australe, N. luteum, N. mediterraneum* and others
- *Neonectria radicicola*
- *Neophaeomoniella niveniae*
- *Phaeoacremonium africanum, P. aleophilum, P. alvesii* and others
- *Phaeomoniella chlamydospora*
- *Phoma cladoniicola, P. incompta*
- *Phomopsis* sp.
- *Phlyctema vagabunda*
- *Pleurostomophora richardsiae*
- *Punctularia atropurpurascens*
- *Pseudophaeomoniella globosa, P. oleae*
- *Pythium irregulare, P. schmitthenner*
- *Sardiniella urbana*
- *Schizophyllum commune*
- *Sclerotium rolfsii*
- *Thelonectria aurea*
- *Trametes versicolor*
- *Ulocladium consortialis*
- *Vredendaliella oleae*
- *Xenocylindrosporium margaritarum* sp. *nov*

Root Dot Diseases

Root rot diseases caused by soil-inhabiting fungi can cause serious problems in olives, including reduced growth, wilting, root necrosis and, in severe cases, dieback or tree death. Severity of root disease appears to depend on climate, soil, site and cultural practices. It can spread through cuttings used for propagation in nurseries.

Transmission: Soil-borne. The fungus survives in soil for many years and can infect the roots of a wide range of plants. It can spread in irrigation water and infected soil on farm machinery and tools.

Phytophthora root rot

Phytophthora acerina, P. bilorbang, P. cactorum, P. cinnamomi, P. citricola, P. crassamura, P. cryptogea, P. drechsleri, P. inundata, P. megasperma, P. nicotianae, P. niederhauserii, P. oleae, P. palmivora, P. pini, P. plurivora, P. pseudocryptogea.

Geographical distribution: Worldwide.

Symptoms: Several *Phytophthora* species of different phylogenetic clades have been reported as causative agents of leaf chlorosis, wilting, defoliation, reduced plant growth and twig dieback, as a consequence of root rot and basal stem cankers on olives. These species differ in aggressiveness, temperature requirements for growth, geographical distribution and ecology.

Transmission: *Phytophthora* is a soil-borne organism, spread by movement of soil, water and infected plants.

Trees infected with *Phytophthora* are consistently associated with excessively wet soils, clay-panning or poor drainage, high relative humidity and mild temperatures occurring in autumn.

The pathogen can live independently in the soil and survive long periods of dryness as oospores or chlamydospores. *Phytophthora* species that infect olives can vary in their aggressiveness and responses to soil moisture and temperature conditions.

In moist environments, some soil-inhabiting species, such as *P. nicotianae* and *P. oleae*, have occasionally adapted to an aerial lifestyle and may infect above-ground parts of olive trees, such as fruits, leaves and twigs, causing fruit rot, leaf drying and twig dieback.

Phytophthora root rot disease.

Verticillium wilt (defoliating strains)
Verticillium dahliae (Kleb.)

Geographical distribution: Widely distributed throughout the Mediterranean olive-growing region.

Damage: The verticillium wilt fungus affects the vascular system, starting in the soil from spores close to a root. The fungus infests the tree from the roots to the leaves, and dead leaves fall to the ground containing spores to continue the cycle of infection.

Symptoms: Darkening or black streaking of xylem tissue resulting in defoliation or rapid shoot death with brown leaves attached. A whole branch is usually affected, indicating the infection is moving up the tree xylem from one or more of the infected roots; ends of branches die.

Transmission: The causal agent *V. dahliae* is a soilborne fungus that penetrates the roots of the host plant and colonises its vascular system. The fungus survives in soil for many years and can infect the roots of a wide range of plants. It can spread in irrigation water and infected soil on farm machinery and tools.

Verticillium on olive trees in Spain. (UNIVERSITY OF CORDOBA)

Damp clay soils with high temperature are especially favourable for infection, such as in irrigated groves. Soils high in organic matter are resistant to verticillium due to the presence of antagonistic microorganisms.

Economic importance: Verticillium wilt is a serious problem and nowadays is considered the main challenge for olive growing. Causes high reduction of yields and tree mortality. The disease incidence and severity are usually highest in young trees. It is one of the major limiting factors of olive-oil production.

Symptoms of *V. dahliae* cause verticillium wilt on young tree.

Charcoal root rot

Macrophomina phaseolina (Tassi) Goid. = *Sclerotium bataticola* (Taubenh).

Charcoal root rot disease is encouraged by stresses such as drought and high temperatures. *Macrophomina phaseolina* occurs in olive propagation materials in nurseries, where it produces small, black, irregular sclerotia on roots (these are survival structures of the fungus). The abundant production of minute black sclerotia of the fungus cause the rotted tissues to become blackened, and for this reason the various diseases are known as charcoal rot. Severely affected roots blacken and rot away. The occurrence of weakly pathogenic strains of *M. phaseolina* on olives has been reported.

Rhizoctonia root rot

Rhizoctonia solani Kühn (teleomorph *Thanatephorus cucumeris* (Frank) Donk)

Rhizoctonia solani is a soil-borne basidiomycete fungus with a necrotrophic lifestyle that causes disease on many economically important crop plants worldwide.

Roots turn brown and outer bark may slough off. Black sclerotia (survival structures) may form on roots. Above-ground symptoms are similar to droughting, and include leaf-tip death, defoliation and plant death.

Young nursery plants are most affected. Healthy mature trees appear to be less susceptible.

R. solani occurs with soil movement, in water, and on contaminated tools and plant parts. *Rhizoctonia* diseases are more severe in soils that are moderately wet rather than waterlogged or dry.

White root rot / Dematophora root rot

Rosellinia necatrix Berl. ex Prill. (anamorph *Dematophora necatrix* R. Hartig)

A well-known and serious ascomycete pathogen for many plant species.

Rosellinia necatrix causes white (or dematophora) root rot, which, by aerial symptoms, shows a progressive weakening of the plant, accompanied by a decline in vigour. The leaves wilt and dry, and the tree can eventually die. White cottony mycelium and mycelial strands can be observed in the crown and on the root surface.

- On woody plant roots, the fungus can be located between the bark and the wood, developing typical mycelium fans, invading the whole root and causing general rotting.
- The whitish mycelial patches of *Rosellinia* resemble those of *Armillaria*, but *Rosellinia* mycelia lack the characteristic mushroom-like odour produced by *Armillaria*.

- The fungus lives as mycelia in roots of infected plants. *Rosellinia* can also persist in soil for several years in dried pieces of infected bark and wood.
- When the soil is moist, and especially if soggy and of moderate temperature, the mycelia grow from infected roots and spread through the soil.

Armillaria root rot, Honey fungus

Armillaria mellea (Vahl) Kummer and *Armillaria luteobubalina* (Watling and Kile)

Armillaria luteobubalina, commonly known as honey fungus, is a species of mushroom in the order Agaricales. The fungus grows in dense clusters and is quite spectacular when it fruits prolifically.

The most distinctive symptoms, found only on closer examination of affected trees, are: rotted roots and stems, creamy-white felt-like areas of fungal mycelium immediately below the bark of infected wood, and dark bootlace-like fungal strands (rhizomorphs), which can sometimes be found growing through the soil and attached to the host roots. The toadstools (the fruiting bodies of the fungus) have honey-coloured to deep brown caps.

Above-ground symptoms on infected plants are: leaf yellowing, stunting, limb dieback and tree death.

White root rot.

Wood Decay Diseases

Basidiomycetes existing on hardwood hosts, including olive species, cause white rot symptoms. White rot is often very prominent in older trees and can degrade all components of cell walls.

In all cases, wood rot attacks occur via wounds and the necrosis usually develops slowly inside the trunk, with the fruiting bodies eventually emerging – they are very clearly noticeable (conks, hard layers) – on the exterior of the tree trunk. In trees severely affected by wood rot, the attack also involves the roots. As large hardwood areas are destroyed, the tree loses its vigour, its senescence accelerates and it may die.

Many species of wood-rotting basidiomycetes are not directly responsible for tree mortality; however, they can lead to structural deterioration of woody tissues and economic damage after several years.

- *Dactylonectria torresensis* (A. Cabral, Rego and Crous)
- *Fomes fulvus* var. *oleae* (Scop)
- *Fomitiporia mediterranea* (Fisch)
- *Phellinus igniarius* (L) Quél.
- *Polyporus* spp.
- *Pseudophaeomoniella oleae*
- *Schizophyllum commune* Fr.
- *Stereum hirsutum* (Willd) S.F. Gray
- *Trametes versicolor* (L.) Lloyd

Mushroom / Tree fungi

Massariella oleae (Corte) [Amphisphaeriaceae]

- *Omphalotus illudens* (Schwein) [Marasmiaceae]
- *Omphalotus olearius* (DC:Fr.) Singer [Marasmiaceae]
- *Pycnoporus cinnabarinus* (Jacquin) Karsten [Polyporaceae]

Omphalotus olearius has been reported in Greece as the cause of 'Gelatina' disease of olive roots. It is a brilliant orange mushroom that usually grows in dense tufts from the decaying underground roots of olive trees.

Omphalotus olearius mushroom. (I. FOIANINI)

Olive tree damaged by sun; *Pycnoporus cinnabarinus* fruiting body is a bright red-orange shelf fungus.

Bacterial Diseases

Olive knot / Tuberculosis

Pseudomonas savastanoi pv. *savastanoi* (Smith) Gardan *et al.* [Pseudomonadaceae]

Geographical distribution: *Pseudomonas savastanoi* pv. *savastanoi*, the bacteria responsible for olive knot, is a serious disease of olives in the Mediterranean region. This bacteria has been detected in 22 countries.
Damage: Olive knot appears as rough galls or swellings on twigs, branches, trunks, roots, fruit and leaves.
Symptoms: The most common symptom is the round tumour or gall – the 'knot' – that may be quite large, measuring several centimetres in diameter. The galls form on the trunk, limbs, stems and shoots. The leaves, roots and crown may be affected, although the infection is less frequent and severe. Fruit is seldom affected. Young galls are greenish or pale brown and smooth. Internally they are spongy and watery. Older galls are darker, their internal tissue is usually hollow and the cover is rough and cracked; insects often settle in these. Severely affected stems are stunted, defoliated and may die.
Transmission: When it rains, the galls ooze infectious bacterial goo that can be transmitted to uninfected plants. Mechanical pruning and harvesting increases damage to trees and the risk of spreading the inoculum from tree to tree.
Economic importance: Olive knot is a devastating disease. The economic significance is evident in its adverse effects on yield, fruit size and fruit quality.

Olive twigs covered by knots, caused by *Pseudomonas savastanoi.*

Olive knots damage fruit stems and fruits.

Crown gall / Neck tumours

Agrobacterium tumefaciens (Smith and Townsend) = *Rhizobium radiobacter* / *Agrobacterium radiobacter* (Beijerinck and van Delden) [Rhizobiaceae]

Geographical distribution: *Agrobacterium tumefaciens* causes crown gall in olive plants in different olive-growing regions around the world.

Symptoms: Crown gall causes rough, woody, tumour-like galls to form on roots, trunks and occasionally branches. Crown gall disease was observed on one-year-old olive plants of the cultivar 'Manzanilla' in Pakistan. Large tumours were evident on the collar region, causing growth stunting, leaf yellowing and overall plant dieback – 25 per cent of the young plants in the orchard had gall formation with size varying from 20–150mm (1–6in).

- Galls can interrupt the flow of nutrients and water within the tree, reducing overall plant growth and vigour.
- Young plants with many galls, and plants with a gall completely encircling the main stem, are the most severely affected and can be killed by the disease.
- Mature trees often tolerate many galls with few negative effects.
- Plants with crown gall are more susceptible to drought stress, winter injury and secondary diseases that enter the plant through cracks in the gall.

Transmission: The pathogen can survive in the soil or inside plants. It can be spread through rain, irrigation water, wind, insects, tools, and use of contaminated soil during propagation or planting. Detached galls that rest on the ground or in the soil are primary inoculum sources. Although the bacterial population will decline in the absence of a host plant, the pathogen may survive in soil for up to three years.

Crown gall on an olive tree.

Crown gall tumour development on an olive tree. (OLIVICOLTURA ITALIANA)

Wound cankers

Xanthomonas campestris, *Ralstonia solanacearum* and *Burkholderia caryophylli*

Symptoms: Leaf wilting, stem cankers and dieback.

Transmission: Bacterial pathogens enter plants through wounds, principally produced by adverse weather conditions, through wounds made at pruning or harvest, or frost and cold injuries that caused stem tissue to crack or peel.

Ralstonia solanacearum, the causal agent of olive bacterial wilt. (FEDERAL UNIVERSITY OF UBERLÂNDIA, BRAZIL)

Bacterial canker case – bacterium *Xanthomonas* sp.

Olive quick decline syndrome (OQDS)

Olive quick decline, *Xylella fastidiosa* subsp. *pauca* (with vectors)

Geographical distribution: Italy, Portugal, France, Spain, and North and South America.

Xylella fastidiosa is a bacterial plant pathogen that affects a wide range of plant species. It is a gram-negative bacterium that resides in the xylem, the water-conducting tissues of plants. This is a bacterial disease spread by insect vectors.

Symptoms: Leaf scorch, wilting, yellowing, stunted growth, and dieback of branches. Symptoms are easily confused with water stress or the presence of other pathogens.

OQDS is a severe disease, caused by strains of *Xylella fastidiosa* subsp. *pauca* in susceptible olive cultivars. Conversely,

resistant olive cultivars do not develop OQDS but present scattered branch dieback, which generally does not evolve to severe canopy decline. Leccino and Fs-17 (= Favolosa®) are two olive cultivars that show significant resistance to the bacteria.
Transmission: *Xylella fastidiosa* is transmitted primarily by xylem-feeding insects, such as sharpshooters and spittlebugs, which acquire the bacterium while feeding on infected plants and then spread it to healthy plants. The bacterium colonises the xylem vessels of the host plant, blocking water transport and disrupting the flow of nutrients, which results in various symptoms and ultimately the decline and death of the infected plant.

There are no known cures for this disease.
Economic importance: OQDS is a serious plant disease, which can lead to significant economic losses in olive culture. In Italy alone, *Xylella* has infected and killed 21 million trees, many of which were several centuries old.

Olive quick decline syndrome, *Xylella fastidiosa*. (UNIVERSITY OF BARI, ITALY)

Olive quick decline syndrome. (EPPO)

Leaf scorch

Scorch is a symptom of plant disease in which tissue is 'burned' because of unfavourable conditions or infection by bacteria or fungi.

'Brusca' (leaf scorch or marginal leaf burn) is a disease of olives typically characterised by the desiccation and death of tissues at the tip and/or along the edge of the leaf blade, which can be followed by defoliation. These studies have established that 'brusca' may have multiple origins which can be divided into 'abiotic brusca' (non-parasitic scorching) and 'biotic brusca' (parasitic scorching).

Parasitic brusca: *Stictis panizzei* De Not. [Syn. *Martamyces panizzei* (De Not.) Minter] = anamorph

Phyllosticta panizzei (Petri).

Weak foliar pathogens (i.e. the discomycete fungus, *Stictis panizzei*) or xylem-invading fungi or bacteria that plug the water conducting vessels can, in principle, be the agents of 'parasitic brusca'.

These agents may include leaf scorch – *Xylella fastidiosa* subsp. multiplex (with vectors) – a xylem-limited bacterium, which has recently been found associated with the disease Olive quick decline syndrome (OQDS).

Non-parasitic brusca: Can be induced by any physical cause that affects water supply to the leaf margin cells (for example, insufficient moisture in the soil, water lost too quickly from the leaves to be replaced adequately, damaged roots, and so on), or by hot dry winds, salty winds, low temperatures or nutrient deficiency/toxicity.

'Non-parasitic brusca' (non-parasitic leaf scorch).
There is no sign of fungal infection on the necrotic leaf tips.

'Parasitic brusca' (parasatic leaf scorch). Necrotic leaf tips show plenty of *Stictis panizzei* apothecia.

Deformation of olive leaves.

Viral Diseases

Like other crops, olives are not free from virological problems. The first report on a probable viral disease of olives was back in 1938, and since then several viruses and virus-like diseases have been reported.

Seventeen viruses are considered as olive-tree pathogens and these have been reported in 22 countries on five continents, showing different symptoms on different olive-tree varieties.

The most viruses have been detected in Italy, Portugal, Spain and the USA. The economic impact of these infections has not really been determined, although recent studies report that some olive viruses seem to affect the oil yield and quality, or market value due to defects in visual attraction.

The 17 olive viruses are as follows:

Olivavirus [Olive leaf yellowing associated virus (OLYaV)]
Nepovirus [Cherry leaf roll virus (CLRV)]
Nepovirus [Arabis mosaic virus (ArMV)]
Necrovirus [Olive latent virus-1 (OLV-1)]
Oleavirus [Olive latent virus-2 (OLV-2)]
Marafivirus [Olive latent virus-3 (OLV-3)]
Cucumovirus [Cucumber mosaic virus (CMV)]
Nepovirus [Strawberry latent ring spot virus (SLRSV)]
Undetermined [Olive semi latent virus (OSLV)]
Alphanecrovirus [Olive mild mosaic virus (OMMV)]
Capillovirus [Olive yellow mottling and decline assosiated virus (OYMDaV)]
Nepovirus [Olive latent ring spot virus (OLRSV)]
Tepovirus [Olive latent T (OlVT)]
Potexvirus [Olive vein yellowing associated virus (OVYaV)]
Necrovirus [Tobacco necrosis virus D (TNV-D)]
Tobamovirus [Tobacco mosaic virus (TMV)]
Nepovirus [Olive latent ringspot virus (OLRSV)]

Sometimes viruses are detected in olive plants that show symptoms, including severely distorted leaves, mishapen fruits, double nodes, fasciation of stems and tree decline. Often, however, viruses occur symptomless. SLRSV was found to be associated with a severe symptomatology of the Italian cultivar 'Ascolana Tenera', consisting of distorted sickle-shaped leaves and fruit deformation. ArMV was isolated from declining trees with sickle-shaped leaves and OLRSV from plants showing partial defoliation. OLV-1 was isolated from an olive tree showing some fascinations and bifurcation of leaves and stems. Some have latent infection that has not been associated with specific disease symptoms, nor with loss of vigour or production. CLRV, CMV and OLV-2 were identified from symptomless trees. The virus (OLV-1) is transmitted by grafting and seed transmission in olives, reported at the rate of 82 per cent. In a new viral species of the genus *Tepovirus* (Betaflexiviridae) T (OlVT), infections remained latent.

Virus and virus-like diseases / Diseases of unknown aetiology

- **Sickle leaf** is one of the most common virus-like diseases of olive trees and has been proven to be graft-transmissible to *Olea europaea*. The nature of the causal agent is, however, still unknown.
- **Vein banding and vein clearing**. Symptoms of vein banding are chlorotic to yellow discolouration along the main veins, low yield, severe defoliation and decline. There is no ultimate proof of the etiological involvement of this virus in the disease.
- **Leaf yellowing** complex apparently corresponds to three different diseases, which are 'olive vein yellowing' (OVY), 'olive leaf yellowing' (OLY) and 'olive yellow mottling and decline' (OYMD). The typical symptoms of the complex are poor fruit set, bright yellow discolouration of the foliage, mottling, necrosis, extensive defoliation and dieback.
- **Bumpy fruits** have been recorded in Italy, Portugal and Turkey. The causal agent of this disorder was accepted as SLRSV (strawberry latent ring spot virus). Bumpy fruit is often associated with severe narrowing and twisting of leaves, bunchy growth and reduced yield.
- **Vegetative disorders** in olive trees: bud failure and formation of sphaeroblasts with rosettes of shoots, bushy growth, shoots with witches' brooms, chlorosis and deformation of the leaves, and flower abortion.
- **Spherosis**. Common symptoms of the disease are dwarfing, low productivity and development of mini-sphaeroblasts on the trunk and branches. Although it is a graft-transmissible disorder and seems to be naturally spreading, the epidemiology and etiology of the disease are still unknown.

Bumpy fruits are a symptom of strawberry latent ring spot virus (SLRSV).

Leaf yellowing virus (OLY).

Olive vein yellowing associated virus (OVYaV).

Phytoplasma Diseases

- Phytoplasmas have been reported on olives in Europe, Asia and Australia.
- Phytoplasmas are essentially tiny specialised bacteria that lack cell walls. They can be difficult to identify because they only survive and reproduce in living plant tissue. For many years, diseases caused by these organisms were thought to result from viruses, because the symptoms appear very similar.
- Phytoplasmas constitute a monophyletic clade within the class Mollicutes. The phytoplasmas identified in olive trees have been classified as Aster yellows group, Elm yellows group, Stolbur group and Stolbur group/witches' broom.

Stolbur: Olive witches' brooms

Vegetative disorders observed in olive tress: abnormal shoots, bushy growth, shortened internodes and proliferation (witches' brooms), formation of sphaeroblasts with rosettes of shoots, leaf deformation and chlorosis, flower abortion and bud failure.

The epidemiology of olive viruses and phytoplasma diseases remains largely unknown. It is essential to use virus-free and healthy propagation material to establish a plantation.

Bushy growth – shoots with witches' brooms on olive trees.

Olive phytoplasma. Vegetative disorders in olive trees include bud failure, the formation of sphaeroblasts with rosettes of shoots, and chlorosis of the leaves.

Tree burrs/burls and Sphaeroblasts

Burrs or burls

A burr or burl is an abnormal growth, which occurs as a swelling growth (knobbly growth) on the lower trunk. They develop as irregular bumps and wart-like outgrowths. While burls usually start out small, they can grow to be quite large. These growths can be located near the roots, in the middle of a tree, or even in a ring all the way around the tree. They consist of a mass of bud and shoot tissue that grows profusely to form a distinctive growth on the trunk. Cambial growth is hyper-stimulated as a way for the tree to isolate the area. Almost all burl wood is covered by bark. Their exact cause is something of a mystery.

- Burrs generally form in response to some form of stress. This could be a wound, maybe caused by human intervention, or some natural occurrence.
- Burrs form over the wound, protecting the tree from any further damage at that particular site. While burrs can appear somewhat unsightly, they don't cause any harm to the tree.
- Some burrs seem to develop from a proliferation of bud tissue that keeps multiplying instead of developing shoots. They are often triggered by environmental conditions, but certain rootstocks and some cultivars are also genetically predisposed to their development.
- Although it is a graft transmissible disorder and seems to be naturally spreading, the epidemiology and etiology of the condition are still unknown.

Sphaeroblasts

A sphaeroblast is a woody extrusion from the trunk or branch of a tree, usually taking the form of a rounded spherical shape. Sphaeroblasts originate from a bud or a cluster of buds (especially adventitious buds) on the trunk or branch that have abnormally generated a rounded layer of cambium and then subsequently thickened to produce wood (xylem), rather than growing shoots or foliage.

Sphaeroblasts.

Microsphaeroblasts.

Burr growing on an olive tree.

Tree trunk that looks like an elephant's foot.

CHAPTER 3

Disorders

Native to the Mediterranean, olive trees flourish in hot, dry summers with low humidity and benefit from cool winters to be more productive. They are rather tolerant of frost and wind, growing well in Mediterranean, temperate, arid, subtropical and coastal areas. Weather is very important for the development of fruits.

Olives are grown not only in cool and dry areas but also under warm and humid conditions. In recent times, olive growing has been introduced into new countries with no previous tradition of olive-oil production.

Some olive trees have adapted to hard climatic zones. They can withstand high salinity in areas close to the sea, the drought of the desert and the cold mountain climate at altitudes of up to 800m (2,600ft).

Although olives are relatively tolerant of drought, as an evergreen tree they require water year-around for commercial production. Low water availability leads to reduced tree growth and lower yields of fruit and oil.

Other factors which affect the growth of olive trees include a lack of or an excess of essential nutrients, or an unsatisfactory environment – it may be too cold or hot, too wet or dry, or too windy. Additionally, there may be unsuitable soil characteristics such as poor physical condition, waterlogging, high salinity, unsuitable pH levels, and so on. Also, pollution in the environment, fire damage, and climatic extremes such as lightning, hail, ice, snow and storms can cause heavy losses to olive trees.

This chapter focuses on the most important disorders of olives caused by environmental, physical and chemical stresses that can affect normal physiological processes in trees.

Abiotic disturbances that have known impacts on olives:

Anthropogenic – fire, air pollution
Climatological – drought
Geophysical – tsunamis, earthquakes
Hydrological – floods and flash floods
Meteorological – cyclones, storms (wind, snow, frost, ice, hail, dust and sand), tornadoes, thunderstorms and lightning

Factors Affecting Pollination and Fruit Set in Olives

Pollination

Olive flowers self-pollinate. The anthers (located at the top of the filaments attached to the stamen) drop pollen on the stigma of the pistil. The pollen grains germinate and olive growth is underway. Although not necessary for pollination, wind and bees may aid in pollination by disturbing the flower, causing pollen to fall from the anther to the stigma. Cross-pollination occurs when wind or a bee transfers pollen from one flower to the stigma of another flower.

Cross-pollination

Although most olive varieties are self-fertile to some extent, research has shown that cross-pollination generally improves the fruit set of most varieties, especially when the environmental conditions are not optimal. Generally having two or three different varieties growing in close proximity (30m) will facilitate adequate cross-pollination.

Arbequina, Pendulino, Coratina, Picual and Manzanillo are some of the main varieties used for cross-pollination. If a tree flowers well in the spring and does not set any fruit it may be an indication that cross-pollination is required.

Irrigation

- It is important to ensure that the trees are not water stressed during the period of flower induction and development, which starts in late autumn and early winter.
- In winter drought conditions, leaf development is favoured at the expense of flower development.
- Water stress during late winter and spring is also a problem, resulting in malfunctioning flowers that do not develop correctly and prematurely drop without setting fruit.

Nutrition

Adequate levels of nutrients, especially nitrogen, calcium and boron, are required for optimal flowering and fruit set.

A leaf analysis taken in mid-summer will give a good indication of a tree's nutritional status and fertiliser requirements. Generally, olives require either manure or other fertiliser on an annual basis for good fruit set.

- It is common for olive growers to apply a foliar spray of boron and calcium in late winter just prior to bud burst to improve fruit set.
- Excessive nitrogen fertiliser may also be a problem with some varieties, especially in warm winter climates, because it tends to encourage excessive vegetative growth through the winter at the expense of floral development.

Environment

- Hot dry winds during flowering are detrimental to pollination/fertilisation.
- Rain during flowering can also disrupt the pollination process.
- Frost and mist in the early stages of development can be a limiting factor in fruit development.
- Some winter chilling is required for flower initiation.
- Growers who intend to plant olives in a warm climate, outside of the traditional climatic zones, should regard the initial planting as a trial and not a commercial venture until varietal performance is proven.

Pests and Diseases

Pest and disease problems can severely affect floral initiation and flowering, for example Anthracnose, Peacock Spot, Scale, and so on.

The general tree stress caused by these problems is detrimental to the flowering process and often causes serious crop failure.

Pruning

If fruit yield has been poor in previous seasons it is recommended to wait until the trees are flowering in spring before pruning. Then, if pruning is required, only prune the branches that are unproductive so that you leave as many flowering branches as possible.

To manage alternate bearing trees – trees bearing large crops one year and none the next – you need to prune heavily in a heavy bearing year and remove clumps of fruit with relatively few leaves – fruit thinning is the only real way to limit alternate bearing.

Flower and Fruit Abortion (Poor Fruit Set)

Various stress factors can inhibit flowers, fruit set and fruit development.

The abortion of flowers and fruits of fruit trees in general is divided into categories:

1. Natural Abortion

This is caused by the large number of flowers that formed and competed among themselves for the water and nutrients inside the tree, and this competition occurs at the beginning of the flowering and fruit-setting periods, so the result is the abortion of large quantities of flowers and the newly set fruits. This does not affect the final yield, because the remaining amount is often sufficient to give the desired yield. It was found that 2 per cent of the total olive flowers are sufficient to give a full commercial crop.

2. Abnormal Abortion

The abnormal abortion (or shedding) of flowers and fruits in general is due to the following reasons:

Environmental Reasons

The most important environmental reasons that cause flowers and fruits to shed are:

- Olive trees require winter cold to achieve normal blooming and fruiting. The optimal degree of cold winters is dependent upon the origin of the olive cultivar (for example, Eastern Mediterranean versus Southern Europe).
- Cold springs will negatively impact harvest by delaying blooming and increasing flower abnormalities. If the temperature drops to just above zero in spring this can damage the ovary and the stylus. Low or high temperatures can cause the death and shed of flowers and fruits. The great difference in temperature between night and day also has an effect on the occurrence of abortions.
- Frost and mist in the early stages of development can be a limiting factor in fruit development.
- Strong winds, especially dusty ones.
- Heavy rain and hail.
- Fruits are exposed to intense direct sunlight, leading to sun blight, which appears in the form of large brown spots and may eventually lead to fruit shedding.
- In shady situations, where insufficient sunlight penetrates the trees, this can lead to flower and fruit abortions.
- High percentage of salts in the soil or in the irrigation water causes general stress for plants and thus the inability to carry out the important vital processes of flowering and fruit setting.
- Drought stress/Lack of soil moisture. Flower buds require an adequate amount of water to support rapid cell expansion. Usually, a mild to moderate water stress will not jeopardise flowers, but a severe water stress can lead to flower bud abortion. Hot windy conditions at flowering time and lack of soil moisture can reduce fruit set. It's crucial to have enough irrigation during flowering and fruit set. Even if trees are irrigated, strong heat will burn the flowers, in dry years tiny fruits can dry up and fall off. Without water, many flowers fall to the ground before they can produce fruit. It's crucial to have enough irrigation during flowering and fruit set.
- One factor influencing pistil abortion in the olive is leaf-bud ratio, or the number of leaves present for each inflorescence bud. If there is a reduction in the number of leaves, poor development of the olive flowers can be expected, and with further loss of leaves, the number of aborted pistils increases.

Mechanical Reasons/Causes

Mechanical flower abortion may occur due to severe air currents resulting from spraying operations, whether for pesticides or nutrients, as a result of using high-pressure spray or increasing pesticide doses to greater than the recommended limit.

Physiological Reasons

Flower abortions may occur due to one or more of the following reasons:

- The lack of pollination and fertilisation in flowers, which leads to their shed. For example, the flowers on the tree may be feminine only (the absence of male flowers) and pollination does not occur.
- A large number of flowers or fruits on the tree increases its abortions, and the reason may be due to competition among them to obtain nutrients such as carbohydrates manufactured by the leaves.
- Lack of fertilisation, especially the lack of nitrogen in the soil, which increases the abortion of flowers and fruits. On the other hand, excessive nitrogen fertilisation leads to weakness in the area of separation, which is the neck of the flower attached to the plant, and fall occurs as a result of this weakness. Also, the lack of interest in fertilising plants with phosphate fertilisers at the required rates leads to a weakness in the plant's energy, its inability to flower well and the dropping of a few flowers.
- Severe deficiency in calcium and boron in plants contributes to abortion, because of the important role of these two elements in the fruit set. Zinc deficiency increases flower and fruit abortion.
- Excessive irrigation leads to a very high level of ground moisture, and consequently suffocation of the roots and poor ventilation, which leads to the fall of flowers due to their extreme sensitivity to any physiological changes that occur on the plant. Severe thirst for the plant leads to the same result.
- The low depth of the soil in which trees are planted, the growth of the root system of the trees is affected, and the flowers and fruits do not get enough nutrients from the soil.
- The poor health of leaves as a result of disease or insect infestation increases flower and fruit abortion.
- Flowers may fall as a result of spraying plants with copper or insecticides during times of high temperatures.
- Flower abortion may occur as a result of the wrong use of plant growth regulators or as a result of the incorrect mixing of pesticides.
- Infection of flowers and fruits with some diseases and insects causes their abortion.
- Fruits left over from the last season.

Poor fruit set as a result of hot and dry weather.

Poor fruit set as a result of rainy weather.

- In the year after a heavy fruit load, flowering can be quite limited. If a high percentage of fruit is left on the tree from the previous season it will inhibit flower development.
- Fruits ripen and fall naturally from trees.

There can be differences in fruit set between varieties of the same species, independent of climate factors. It is possible to find **two types of fruits**:

1. Typical olive fruits

For fruit to persist, vascular connections must be in place, raw materials must be available and pollination and fertilisation must occur. The fruits are of normal size and characteristics and contain a seed.

Mature olive trees, at a planting density of 250 trees per hectare, produce about 500,000 flowers each. In excess of 98 per cent of these flowers abscise, and only 1.2–2 per cent of the population are required as fruit to establish a commercial crop.

A large population of flowers and fruit cause a drain on tree reserves, make fruit persistence uncertain and inducing an alternate bearing.

2. Shotberries or Parthenocarpic Olives

Productivity in olives is often reduced by the occurrence of parthenocarpic fruitlets known as shotberries. Olive shotberries are small, commonly seedless fruit expressing quantitative parthenocarpy. Commonly known as 'zofairones', they are fruits developed without fertilisation of the egg or the result of an ovarian abortion due to incompatibility of pollen and stigma.

They are small spherical or ovoid fruits, which soon stop growing. They usually fall down before the ripening, although some of them persist in the plant together with the typical fruits.

Sometimes the pollen may not fertilise the ovule but gives the stimulus to the ovary to grow its wall and form a very small fruit (pseudodrupe) with an empty stone, called a 'passerina olive'. These parthenocarpic fruits (from the Greek: *parthénos*, meaning 'virgin', and karpós, meaning 'fruit') normally ripen before harvesting and usually fall before harvesting.

Reasons for the formation of shot-berries can be different, and include: low temperature at the time of flowering; dehydration of the stigma; excessive humidity or high temperatures; genetic reasons; and nutritional deficiencies, from polyamines to problems linked to the vitality of the pollen, especially in self-pollination.

Shotberries or parthenocarpic olives.

Yellow leaves and Leaf drop

Healthy olive leaves are dark green due to a special pigment called chlorophyll. Chlorophyll absorbs sunlight, which the plant uses to grow. When photosynthetic plants lack chlorophyll, their leaves turn yellow. Chlorosis is the scientific term that describes the yellowing of leaves.

A number of factors may trigger chlorosis, including soil pH, nutrient availability and improper watering. Additionally, weather conditions, diseases and pests can cause large-scale yellowing and drop in olive leaves.

Fruit blemishes

Multiple factors are involved in causing rind blemishes (a wide range of scratches and marks on the fruits), which can be generally grouped as biotic and abiotic in nature.

Abiotic factors include environmental (wind, dry branch rub, sunburn), physical and nutritional imbalance, while **biotic** factors include various pests (such as thrips or mites) and diseases, or scratching and feeding damage by birds which downgrades the external quality of the fruit.

Fruit blemishes.

Russet

Russet occurs when the outermost (epithelial) cells of the fruit are injured and callus cells form, producing an injury similar to scab. High humidity levels or the fruits being continually wet, and associated high daytime temperatures and low night temperatures during the fruit development phase, are most commonly associated with the onset of russet. Russet may also be associated with strong winds, when immature fruits rub against other fruit, leaves or stems.

Russet.

Meteorological factors

Olive disorders can be linked to events such as cyclones, storms (wind, snow, frost, ice, hail, dust and sand), tornadoes, thunderstorms and lightning.

Wind

Olive trees have strong trunks, branches and leaves that can resist moderate winds, but strong winds and storms are common and often cause tremendous damage to individual trees. These storms can cause weakly attached branches to break off and rip trees apart or even uproot the tree from the ground. Additionally, wind tends to have a mechanical and dehydrating action on the tree foliage.

The effects of wind include:

- Strong winds cause trees to sway, pulling and stretching their roots. The movement disrupts root-soil contact, decreasing water absorption and increasing the severity of water stress in trees. During severe storms even large trees be simply blown over by a gust of wind.
- Hot and dry winds in spring can affect the biological processes of fertilisation.
- Reduced fruit quality if the wind causes it to rub against twigs or the sharp edges of withered leaves, both of which can cause scratches.
- Cold winds can cause sudden temperature drops, while hot winds can cause burns in apical leaves and damage to flowers and fruits.
- Strong winds can break shoots and branches and drop flowers and fruits.
- Marine winds, transporting salt, can exert a caustic action on leaves and young shoots.

Bora

This phenomenon occurs when the wind causes a turbulent sea and lifts drops of seawater, creating a 'sea smoke'. After the water evaporates from these droplets, a thin layer of salt remains that settles on the soil, grass, shrubs and trees. Salt is especially harmful to young olive trees. As a result, they may remain small and without leaves, while others are killed.

If it does not rain soon after the bora, to wash away the salt, defoliation occurs. The olive trees lose their leaves and have to spend their energy in the following year exclusively on renewing the leaf mass, so there is no yield or a minimal one.

Olive trees blown over during storms.
(I. VLATKOVIC)

Olive tree damage caused by wind.

Dust storms

Wind with dust from deserts seriously and adversely harms the tissues of the plant. Dust accumulation on leaf surfaces induces water stress-like conditions, such as a reduction of stomata conductance, photosynthesis and transpiration, and increased leaf temperature.

Dust storm at an olive grove in Australia.

Dust on olive leaves in Australia.

Lighting strikes

Trees struck by lightning can show damage in a host of different ways. Lightning can blow off a strip of bark, the trunk may be blown apart or partially burnt, or it can develop a crack and burn from the inside out. Often the reason that the entire trunk does not catch fire is that there is considerable amount of moisture content just below the bark.

A tree hit by lightning could conceivably go on to grow normally (depending on the severity of the internal damage), but subtle signs of an internal problem might include leaf wilt or sparse growth.

Ice storms

Ice storms, also historically referred to as glaze storms, are characterised by freezing rain. The raindrops move into a thin layer of below-freezing air right near the surface of the Earth, allowing them to freeze on contact with the ground, trees or other objects. These storms cover trees in a thick layer of ice, adding weight that branches may not be able to support, resulting in branch breakage.

Trees are damaged during ice storms for a number of reasons. The severity of damage and failure of parts of a tree or a whole tree depend on three factors: amount of accumulated ice, exposure to the wind, and duration of the storm. Further, the susceptibility of a particular tree can be affected by tree height and diameter, and characteristics such as weak branch junctures, decaying or dead branches, increased surface area of lateral branches, a broad or unbalanced crown, restricted or unbalanced root systems, and shallow rooting.

Ice on olive tree. (OLIVICOLTURA ITALIANA)

Ice on olive fruits and leaves. (JOHN SYMINGTON)

Freezing fog, Hoar frost and Rime ice

This phenomenon is called freezing fog and the ice crystals that it forms are called rime ice. Hoar frost can look very similar to rime ice but hoar frost forms when the water vapour in the air turns directly to ice crystals without first condensing into water droplets. This can occur on cold, clear nights. Rime ice forms from fog (freezing fog).

Olive fruits with hoar frost.

Snow and Snow storms

A snow storm is a heavy fall of snow that is blown by strong winds. Although snow is generally infrequent in areas where olives are grown, it occasionally creates problems. The snow itself does not represent a serious problem to olive trees, but if it is too abundant, it can cause the breakage of branches, especially if the foliage is quite thick and the main branches have a wide insertion angle on the trunk.

Snow on an olive tree. (OLIVICOLTURA ITALIANA)

Hail storms

Hail is always harmful, but it can cause the greatest damage during phases of flowering and fruit growing and ripening. Hail does not only produce direct damage, breaking the inflorescences and the shoots and injuring the branches and the fruits, but also indirect

Following hail, fruit and twigs may exhibit open, ragged-edged wounds in the skin or bark.

damage because, through wounds to the wood, it can lead to the penetration of bacterial infections such as olive knot disease.

Fruits and twigs may exhibit open, ragged-edged wounds in the skin or bark. The major effect is the destruction of non-lignified tissues. The intensity and timing of the hailstorm determines the magnitude of the losses.

Frost

The sensitivity of olive trees to the cold is affected by several factors, such as cultivar variety, the vegetation stage of the tree, exposure area, air and ground humidity, and the period of the year in which the temperature drops.

Frost thresholds for olives

Frost damage is a time and temperature relationship. Fruit and shoots need time to decrease in temperature to reach freezing point.

- Olive fruit damaged at below −1.7°C (28.9°F);
- Young olive trees and branches can be killed below −5.5°C (22.1°F); and
- Mature trees can be killed at temperatures below −9.5°C (14.9°F), although the cultivars Ascolano, Mission, Barouni and Sevillano are the hardiest and can survive until around −18°C (−0.4°F).

Frost symptoms and outcomes on olives

During late winter and early spring, sharp temperature changes between day and night can cause damage. Frost can seriously harm young shoots and inflorescences, especially in young trees, resulting in serious losses. It can also damage fruit and lead to tip burn, leaf curl, defoliation, limb die-back and bark splitting. The most common issues, however, are damage to spring shoots from late frosts and to late-ripening fruit from early frosts.

Frost damage in young olive trees is similar to sunburn. Young, rapidly growing trees may also develop superficial growth cracks when the inner bark expands faster than the outer bark during periods of optimum growing conditions (the sloughing off of outer bark may accompany trunk expansion; and the outer bark can peel upward). This doesn't cause death right away but it allows bacteria to begin compromising the bark and vascular system, increasing susceptibility to olive knot. The tree becomes weakened and can die eventually.

When frosts are severe they can cause shoots to die and leaves to dry out completely, similar to Verticillium wilt symptoms, although they can be distinguished by their darker colour.

Frost-damaged trunk.
(JONATAN BRUNI)

Frost-damaged bark and burned olive-shoot tips and leaves.

Frost-damaged olive fruits.

Frost-damaged bark and burned olive-shoot tips and leaves.

Buds and flowers

If olive trees are subjected to frost, this can cause the bud to 'burn' when it is forming. With spring around the corner, this means that the harvest will be diminished. Flower damage is often hard to identify. Evidence of frost damage over the winter is that you get to spring and there are no flowers on the trees. The problem can be compounded, though, when olive growers don't realise what has

Frost-damaged olive tree.

happened. When not monitoring temperatures and observing damaged flowering buds, it is easy conclude that this a consequence of last year's over-crop, or drought, or other factors, and miss the fact that there were several nights or mornings when it got too cold and the flowering buds were damaged. If buds are protruding more than 5mm (0.2in) it is likely that frost damage will occur at –2°C (28.4°F).

Shrivelling or roughening of the fruit caused by low temperatures

Early frosts may affect olive fruit, leading to significant changes in the chemical and organoleptic make-up, affecting oil quality and fruit quality for table olives. In extreme situations frost can lead to total crop failure. In areas where there is a risk of autumn frosts, it is preferable to complete harvesting early, to minimise frost damage to olives, which could cause a serious sensorial defect to the oil ('freeze injuries'). Even light frost damage can completely ruin a crop.

- Internal browning begins in the flesh around the pit and radiates outward toward the skin as time progresses. Skin browning indicates an advanced stage and/or greater severity of chilling injury. Lesions increase susceptibility to fungal infection (anthracnose and alternaria).
  Chilling injury can be a major cause of deterioration if fresh olives are stored before processing for longer than two weeks at 0°C (32°F), or five weeks at 2°C (35.6°F).
- Apical end rot (soft nose) disorder is associated with shrivelling of the apical end of the fruit, or the whole fruit, mostly close to harvest. This chilling injury may result from sudden changes in humidity and temperature, for example from 7°C (44.6°F) to –1.5°C (29.3°F). The internal flesh and stone may be blackened throughout the whole fruit or only at the apical end; secondary fungal rots, such as Alternaria species, commonly infect the damaged fruit.
  Symptoms may not be visible externally on olive fruits. Detection and diagnosis of chilling injury is often difficult. The degree of chilling and frost injuries depend on the duration of the cold temperatures and how fast the temperature dropped.
- Brown rot frost injuries to olive fruits occurs with temperatures of –1.7°C (28.9°F). This causes surface blisters and spots, indicating damage around the pit. Depending on the characteristics of the frost, the damaged fruit turns a brownish colour and attains an aqueous consistency before it drops, or it dehydrates, remaining shrivelled until harvested.
  Even light frost damage can completely ruin a crop.

Secondary fungal rots, such as *Alternaria* species, commonly infect the damaged fruits.

Brown rot frost injury shrivels or roughens the fruit.

Anthropogenic factors

Fire

Drought and very high summer temperatures may result in severe fires. Olive growers have recorded severe losses due to fires. Damage tends to occur principally to the foliage of the canopy in groves which were bearing full crops, rather than to the bases or trunks of the trees. Complete death of olive trees from wildfire is more likely to occur in younger plantations that have a majority of trees with a stem diameter of less than 20mm (0.8in).

Particularly damaging in many Mediterranean countries is the destruction of monumental trees that have great historical and landscape value. The worst scenario for these plants is when fire burns their decayed wood, which is generally present in the inner part of the trunk; the trees collapse and new sprouts may grow after varying lengths of time, which can be anywhere between a few weeks or one to two years from the event.

Fire damage can lead to the production of abundant suckers from which new plants can be rapidly grown.

Olive trees damaged as a result of fire.

Post-fire regrowth sees the proliferation of suckers around the base of the trunk. (BRETT WORTHINGTON)

Air and soil pollution

Olive trees growing close to cities are continuously exposed to air pollution. Therefore, olive fruits are contaminated by the chemical pollution, which affects the quality of olive oils. Pollution negatively affects the oxidative stability and nutritional value of olive oil, especially by decreasing the contents of antioxidant compounds and the fatty acid composition.

Phytotoxicity may be a result of pesticide spray damage.

Pollutants can also damage plants, causing necrotic grey, light brown or reddish areas on leaves, with young fruit developing brown spots of 1mm (0.04in) in diameter with a slightly sunken surface.

The quality of olive products can be affected by contaminated soil through various mechanisms. One of the main concerns is the leaching of heavy metals, such as nickel (Ni), from soils that accept olive-oil mill waste. To ensure food security and wastewater use for irrigation, monitoring and control of pollution is required.

Climatological factors

Drought

The olive tree is considered to be drought tolerant. However, even though it adapts well to dry climates, if it lacks water for too long, this can lead to serious damage. The young leaves dehydrate and the fruits fall, don't grow, or the growth slows down. Shoot growth is very sensitive to water shortage and is economically significant, since it has an effect on the non- fruit-bearing period of the trees; trunk expansion is also reduced.

The reduced growth rate is attributed to the lower photosynthetic rates due to stomatal closure and also to the reduced functionality of the root system, which is unable to supply the canopy with minerals and water.

Olive trees are highly resistant to water scarcity, but when droughts become extreme the trees activate mechanisms to protect themselves. They don't die, but they no longer produce anything.

Shrivelling and drying of olive fruit

Lack of water during crucial periods of fruit development can cause the fruit to shrivel and dry. Water stress leads to a slow decline in fruit size, where the fruits don't grow and young leaves dehydrate.

High temperatures and lack of water during summer months will certainly impact the tree, resulting in dry olive fruits on trees.

The effects of a high-temperature environment are genotype dependent and in general high temperatures during fruit development affected three important traits: fruit weight, oil concentration and oil quality.

High temperatures of 30–40°C (86–104°F) and lack of water cause the olive fruit to 'wrinkle' and turn black before the date of picking. Such conditions are frequently associated with high vapour pressure deficits between leaves and this may compromise the oil accumulation potential of the olive trees. This condition is reversible, as after rain or irrigation the fruit return to normal, with no browning internally.

Shrivelling of fruits is due to water stress.

A dried olive on a branch – a result of heatwave and drought. (UNIVERSITY OF CORDOBA)

Pit burn. Affected fruit have a normal external appearance but the flesh tissue is brown and discoloured.

Pit burn

High temperatures coinciding with excess soil moisture between early fruit ripening and harvesting may render the fruit susceptible to pit-burn disorder, with softening and brown discolouration of the flesh adjacent to the stone.

Sunburn and sunscald

Trees: Sunburn is a physiological problem. Usually sunburn in trees occurs when the sun causes serious damage to the bark of the trunk or branches.

The tree tissue browns, dies, dries and splits, with the bark peeling back to expose the wood below. Damage can be extensive, or even fatal for some young trees.

Drought and water stress can increase the incidence and severity of sunburn and sunscald.

Sunburned branches may occur after heavy pruning and exposure to the sun.

If the damage is severe enough, sunburn kills the bark causing necrosis – the death of cells or tissue. The lifting and cracking of the bark may lead to attack by insects and fungus.

Fruits: While olives generally thrive in hot climates, their fruiting structures can be very sensitive to solar stress when temperatures rise above 40°C (104°F). Injured olive fruit cortex tissue is tan/brown with firm patches. The discolouration usually does not extend deep into the flesh; it only affects the skin. Sunscalded fruit is unmarketable.

Sunscalded fruits.

Sunburned young leaves.

Sunburned tree bark.

Soil degradation and Soil erosion

Soil degradation and soil compaction are systematically quoted as one of the major threats to the sustainability of olive cultivation. Most frequently the former refers to soil erosion, but it can also mean a decrease of soil nutrients and organic matter. Losses of top soil in areas characterised by shallow soils means a reduction of soil water-storage capacity, which is critical for the survival and productivity of rain-fed olives. The issue threatens olive cultivation either by yield decrease or by the increasing production costs requires to compensate this degradation with additional inputs.

There are two major causes of **soil cracking**: one is climate and the other is anthropogenic activity, include land-use change, land management, land degradation, soil sealing and mining. In most cases, cracking is caused by dryness as well as soil type. Soils go through dry spells when they receive little or no water. Most soils can withstand dry spells without ill effect. However, those consisting of clay soil may crack when severely dehydrated for a prolonged length of time.

Cracking soil in an olive grove as a result of dry weather conditions.

Cracking soil in an olive grove.

Erosion and loss of soil fertility. (SUSTAINOLIVE)

Soil erosion. (ARTEMI CERDÁ, UNIV. VALENCIA)

Salinity

Salinity affects yields. Olives are moderately salt tolerant, although salinity may be a problem when there is a high salt concentration in the soil and/or irrigation water. Olive orchards growing along the coast must also cope with salt deposited by sea winds.

Hydrological factors

Overwatering and high rainfall

The olive tree is adapted to conditions of extreme drought, being able to survive and produce fruit on arid terrain. However, excess moisture in the soil, far from producing benefits, can end up suffocating the roots of the olive tree. These roots can be a focus of rot where fungi and bacteria develop easily. The sensitivity of the olive tree to overwatering depends on the variety, although in general its tolerance is low. However, an olive tree can recover quickly if the waterlogging is temporary.

Flooding

Flooding may cause direct damage to trees and also can weaken trees, making them more susceptible to damage from insects and diseases. It can cause fruit loss and increase the incidence of fruit and root rot diseases, and ultimately there can be tree death due to lack of oxygen in the root zone.

Soil compaction is deleterious because, decreasing permeability, it increases the risk of erosion in hilly areas or stagnant water on plains, and causes root asphyxia due to the lack of oxygen and the accumulation of substances (for example, ethylene) that inhibit root development. It results in reduced plant vigour and productivity, leaf yellowing, root rot, and so on.

Flooding as a result of heavy rain.

Irrigation

Ageing pipes and splits in pipes are common irrigation issues. Blockages are common, especially after the wet season when ants or sediment can build up in the pipes. Be sure to flush out your irrigation system once every couple of weeks in the wet to keep pipes clear.

Irrigation system damage.

Effects of overwatering on fruit

- Leaves and fruits turn brown and drop prematurely. Overwatering damage to fruit can occur after large amounts of spring and summer rain and /or flooding.
- Olive fruit split skin. Lack of water at an early stage followed by a sudden growth spurt can cause the skin on olive fruits to split and fall off the tree. This is as a result of variations in the water supply available at the roots. Rot may subsequently take hold.

Damaged olive fruits and leaves resulting from high rainfall/ flooding.

Olive fruit with split skin as a result of over-irrigation.

Water-logging / Root asphyxiation

This occurs when roots cannot respire due to excess water in the soil. The deficiency of oxygen around the roots linked to waterlogged conditions can cause serious injuries to olive trees.

Olive tree root asphyxiation can be a major problem in heavy ground and soil near wetlands. Waterlogging alters some metabolic functions of the roots, resulting in reduced absorption and transport of water and nutrients. In turn, this causes the soil to stagnate and prevents root growth.

Water-logging leads to root asphyxiation, dry fruits and curled and twisted dry leaves.

Symptoms:

- Plants may look like they need water because symptoms include yellowing leaves that wither and drop off. Wilting of the plant also occur.
- Young stressed plants may show curled and twisted dry leaves.
- The surface of the soil is soaking wet with puddles on it.
- When lifted, the plant roots are black, soft and soggy, and the soil smells of rotten eggs or mushroom compost.
- Plant growth is stunted or plants fail to sprout and shoots die back. Fruits shrivel.
- Waterlogging and compaction can create ideal conditions for diseases such as phytophthora and other fungal attacks.

Wetwood

- When the wood of an olive tree becomes soaked with water and colonised by bacteria it turns dark brown.
- Watering/irrigation will have detrimental effects on the tree, especially when sprinklers are close. If too much water is held close to the bottom of an olive tree this can cause bark splitting.
- The tops of the leaves turn yellow then brown. The leaves then fall.

This doesn't cause death right away but it allows bacteria to begin compromising the bark and vascular system. This does eventually kill a tree by causing it to become weakened and susceptible to wind damage and then insect damage. Once a tree is affected by wetwood, there is no way to eliminate it.

Longitudinal bark splitting on a young olive trunk associated with prolonged exposure to wet soil. This condition is known as 'wetwood'.

Girdling roots

Another symptom, common on many woody plants, that in some way is linked to water stress is girdling roots, or 'encircling roots'. It is a disorder of the root architecture in which roots of affected plants begin to grow circularly around the main stem of the tree, thus cutting off or restricting the movement of water, plant nutrients and stored food reserves. Trees can slowly weaken and die over a period of years or decades.

Poor soil structure, limited soil depth, clay pans, hardpans and poor ground preparation are at the basis of poor drainage, leading to waterlogging and girdling roots. It is advisable to locate olive plantations in places where inundation does not occur, or where raised tree lines, the surface or deep drains can rapidly shed the water.

The sensitivity of the olive tree to pooling depends on the variety, although in general tolerance is low. However, olive trees can recover quickly if the waterlogging is temporary.

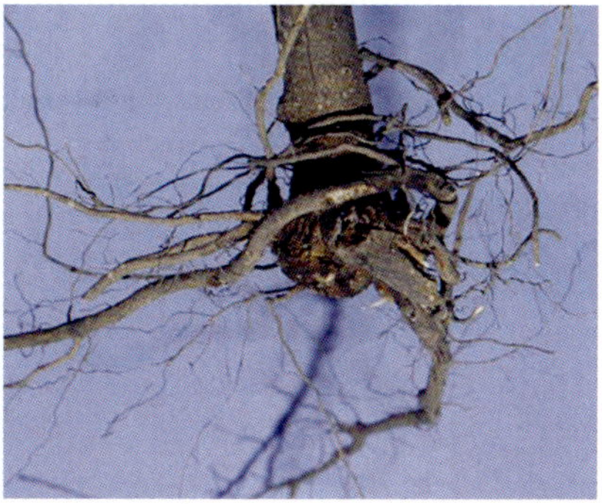

Girdling roots.

Bark splitting

Excessive watering will have detrimental effects on the tree, especially when sprinklers are close. Too much water held at the bottom of olive tree can cause bark splitting. Root rot, such as Armillaria, or bacteria can cause the bark to peel around the base of the tree. The vascular system just below the bark is the most critical part of the entire tree. Serious bark splits may occur due to frost. The sun causes sunburn, which damages the tree significantly. Another potential cause could be a lightning strike if the tree bark is peeling from above and coming down the trunk.

Fog and Relative humidity

High air humidity, more frequent in valley bottoms (as fog), near rivers and lakes and in coastal areas, creates favourable conditions for attacks by pests. Therefore, in sites characterised by high humidity, it is necessary to choose cultivars with good tolerance to potential pests.

Fog, mist or heavy dew can increase the spread the diseases among olives, especially anthracnose, which is the most important fungal disease of olive fruits worldwide.

Fog in an olive grove. (JOHN SYMINGTON)

Rain, heavy dew, mist or fog can increase the spread the disease.

Geophysical factors

Events such as earthquakes and tsunamis can sometimes affect olive trees. For example, an olive grove in Turkey was badly affected by a 7.8-magnitude earthquake that hit on 6 February 2023. The earthquake's sheer power split the olive grove into two and it is now divided by a canyon that is 300m (900ft) wide and 1.5km (0.9 miles) long.

Canyon created by an earthquake in Turkey in 2023. (OGUZ YETER / ANADOLU AGENCY VIA GETTY IMAGES)

Weeds and Spray damage

- A weed is a plant growing where it is not wanted. Weeds provide a home for pests (such as insects and their eggs and larvae) and diseases (for example, fungal spores) during spring and summer, which can then affect an olive crop.
- Weeds compete with trees for water, nutrients and sunlight, potentially hindering their growth and overall health, and interfering with harvesting.
- Dry weed growth is also a fire hazard.

Weeds in an olive grove. (JOHN SYMINGTON)

Spray Damage

Fruits, trunks and leaves can be damaged by incorrect or injudicious use of insecticides, fungicides or herbicides. Copper in excessive dosages can cause necrosis of young sprouts, especially when applied at the beginning of their development. Damage can occur when chemicals are mixed through the application of a number of incompatible pesticides. Glyphosate is commonly applied as an herbicide in olive groves, and glyphosate damage has been recorded, particularly

Fungicide spray damage.

in young trees. The main cause of leaf burn is from spraying onto plant foliage in hot sunny weather during the middle of the day in direct sunlight. The overdosing of chemicals can also be a cause of leaf burn or damage.

One detrimental effect of overfertilising is that it can lead to excessive foliage growth, which requires heavy, time-consuming pruning to bring the tree back into balanced production.

Herbicide spray damage.

Mechanical Damage

Harvester damage is sometimes an issue. Mechanical tree shakers and mechanical pruning may damage the trees if not operated correctly.

High pesticide and herbicides levels can become toxic to roots.

Mechanical tree shakers can damage the tree if not operated correctly.

Nutrient Deficiencies

Intensification of olive orchard management entails increased use of fertilisers, especially nitrogen, phosphorus and potassium. Nutrient deficiency impairs production, whereas overfertilisation may reduce yields and oil quality, and increase environmental hazards and production costs.

What nutrients do plants lack?

Nutrition is an important component of plant health. A nutrient deficiency will reduce a plant's ability to complete its lifecycle of producing flowers and fruits.

Abnormal chemo-physical conditions of the ground or wrong fertilisers could cause the lack of main nutrients – Nitrogen (N), Potassium (K) and Calcium (Ca) – and this could alter the growth and/or the biology of the tree. In particular, nutrients could affect the disease tolerance or resistance of plants to pathogens. In the olive tree the most typical damage due to lack of nutrients is the lack of Boron (B).

What causes plants to have nutrient deficiencies?

Nutrient deficiency may occur due to one or more of the following reasons:

- The soil or growth medium is deficient in the required nutrient.
- The soil is not sufficiently moist to allow the roots to take up and transport the nutrients.
- Some nutrients, for example, are more available to the plant at certain pH levels. Very acid or alkaline conditions, dryness and waterlogging can all make it difficult for plants to take up soil nutrients.
- The nutrient is unable to reach the organ where it is needed most.
- A too-high concentration of one nutrient may outcompete the uptake of a similar nutrient.

What does a nutrient-deficient plant look like?

Boron (B) deficiency is manifested by apical and marginal chlorosis in leaves that end up drying and showing a chlorotic zone between the dry part and the still green part of the leaf, and also in reduced blossoming and fruit development. Boron deficiency may cause the deformation of green fruits, premature fruit drop and poor fruit-set, while brown sunken areas may develop on the fruit, in a symptom called 'monkey face'.

Boron availability by plants decreases under drought conditions and as soil pH increases, particularly in calcareous soils.

To avoid the lack of this nutrient, this microelement should be added by fertilising the leaves.

Nitrogen (N) deficiency is indicated when the leaves are yellowish and become pale; normally this appears first in old leaves. Also, there is heavy defoliation and growth on leaves and shoots is reduced, leading to small trees with poor fruit set and yield.

Potassium (K) deficiency symptoms are similar to those created by tissue dehydration. Leaf tips and margins show progressing chlorosis with subsequent necrosis. Leaf drop gives the branch a bald appearance. There is dull, light brown and sharply delimited necrosis of leaf tips. Potassium deficiency represents the major nutritional disorder in olives growing both in drylands and on calcareous soils, due to its interaction with water shortages and calcium.

Phosphorus (P) deficiency, when severe, causes leaves to develop a purple tint at their tips.

Magnesium (Mg) deficiency results in chlorosis at the tips and margins of the leaves; this advances in the interveinal fields towards the base. A green spot at the base of the leaf remains, sometimes in a triangle from along the midrib, but often more diffuse. Symptoms normally appear first in mature leaves.

Calcium (Ca) deficiency in olives shows as chlorosis in the tips of the leaves, which may extend up to the middle of the leaf; it appears first in young leaves. This deficiency also reduces the consistency of the fruit's tissues. Calcium deficiency is expected in acidic soils. The root systems may show poor growth, and root apexes may appear gelatinous.

Manganese (Mn) deficiency causes leaves show marginal chlorosis, with the tissue surrounding the leaf veins remaining green. It usually appears in middle-aged leaves.

Copper (Cu) deficiency is rarely observed in olives, probably because copper is used as a fungicide to control fungal and bacterial diseases. Periodical Cu sprays also explain its accumulation in the oldest leaves. Symptoms of copper deficiency are characterised by short internodes and leaf chlorosis.

Iron (Fe) deficiency has led to chlorosis being reported in trees growing in calcareous soils in Spain and Israel. Symptoms develop first in young leaves, starting with general chlorosis on the leaves, and may end in necrosis in cases of severe deficiency. Young leaves usually show a reduced size and more extensive yellowish aspects. Fruits are pale and small.

Zinc (Zn) deficiency is rare, although it has been observed in some areas of Turkey, Sicily and Israel, particularly in locations with calcareous soils. Symptoms consist of smaller leaves, twigs with short internodes, young shoots with a compact chlorotic vegetation, and very small terminal leaves that, after showing scattered necrosis, die and drop.

Boron deficiency – note chlorotic halo between dry apical zone and still-green limbus.

Boron nutritional disorder on fruits.

Phosphorus deficiency.

Nitrogen deficiency.

Magnesium deficiency on a leaf showing a pale green colour; gradually the symptom can extend to the whole leaf blade.

Potassium deficiency.

Iron deficiency in olive leaves.

Sap, Gummosis, Sooty Mould, Green Mould, Lichens, Algae and Mosses

Sap

Sap is a solution of water and minerals; the fluid may contain a variety of organic and inorganic compounds, mainly sugars, mineral nutrients, potassium and calcium. Sap is a fluid transported in xylem cells or phloem sieve tube elements of a plant. These cells transport water and nutrients throughout the plant.

Sap-loss of water by automatic irrigation, dripping from the tree after heavy rains following a dry period.

Ooze seeping from tree with stains of black sooty mould associated with sap.

Sap from olive fruit stem. (UNIVERSITY OF CORDOBA)

Sap from olive leaves and trunk.

Gummosis

Oozing sap (gummosis) is a non-specific condition where sap leaks from a wound in the tree. It usually occurs when the tree has a perennial or bacterial canker, or is attacked by borers. If borers dig into sap-producing parts of the wood, the sap flows out of the tunnel. You may also see frass in the oozing sap. However, gummosis can also be caused by any wound, including winter damage, disease damage or damage from a gardening tool.

Symptoms of gummosis include the exuding of amber gum from the trunk or branches of a tree. The gum hardens with time. The tree will usually have other symptoms, including death of one or more branches and yellow leaves. Death of the entire tree may take one to seven years.

Oozing sap (gummosis) from an olive tree trunk, caused by bark borer damage in Calabria, Italy. (D. RAO)

Oozing sap (gummosis). (SIMONE BARRI)

Oozing sap (gummosis) seeping from tree after pruning, with stains of black sooty mould associated with sap.

Sooty mould

The causal agents of this disease are various ascomycete and hyphomycete fungi, particularly species of the *Capnodium*, *Limacinula* and *Aureobasidium* genera and especially the species *C. elaeophilum*. They cause damage to leaves, branches, trunks and fruit.

Most of the fungi comprising the hyphal mass have dark mycelium and spores, which appear dull black to the unaided eye. This black layer easily comes off with the finger; it consists of mycelium and spores of pathogen fungi that live saprophytically on the external parts (exopathogens), using sugary substances ('honeydew') produced usually by the black scale (*Saissetia oleae*) or sometimes by the tree when under stress conditions involving wounding and subsequent release of sap on the bark. Wounding can be caused by sapsuckers or small rodents, frost cracking or water stress with subsequent release during early spring of large quantities of sap containing a relatively high sugar concentration. The sap saturates the bark, providing a food base for the fungi.

The mould persists on stems and twigs of woody plants and is renewed from existing parts of the fungus produced the previous season. Warm temperatures and dry weather increase the prevalence of sooty moulds. Sooty mould can interfere with plant photosynthesis, reducing tree vigour and yield, tainting the oil, increasing fruit washing costs at harvest, and increasing spray costs.

Sooty mould on olive fruits and leaves.

Sooty mould on olive leaves caused by scale insects.

Green mould

Green mould grows on the leaves of olive trees planted in situations that are too wet, such as close to creeks. Too much moisture on the leaves and stems leads to green mould.

Green mould on olive leaves.

Green bark on olive trees

Olive-tree bark can range in colour depending on the season, and is more variable on younger bark. If a tree naturally has green bark, it means that there is chlorophyll present in the tree bark. Chlorophyll is a natural pigment that gives plants and algae their green colour. It is also an essential element of photosynthesis. Lenticel openings on the bark allow for gas exchange to facilitate photosynthesis. Green bark on an olive tree can be the result of defoliation caused by peacock spot disease.

Green bark on olive tree resulting from defoliation caused by peacock spot disease.

Lichens, algae and mosses

Lichens, algae and mosses grow profusely on the trunks, limbs and twigs of many trees and shrubs. Cool, cloudy, wet weather is ideal for these organisms.

Lichens have two components – a fungus and an alga living in association with one another to give the appearance of a single plant. They occur in several forms, such as crusty grey, green, yellow and white growths. Some are leaf-like, others resemble a tuft of horse hair hanging from the branches. Many lichens are more evident on stressed tree trunks. Lichens tend to grow on trees that are declining, so their appearance is a sign that something is wrong with the tree.

Mosses are green plants somewhat similar to algae except they have a complex structure that resembles stems and leaves.

Algae favour trees affected by poor nutrition, poor growing conditions and other stresses such as a dense canopy or a wet and humid environment.

All these primitive plants contain chlorophyll and make their own food, so they do not directly injure the plants on which they grow. At times, however, the growth becomes objectionable or unsightly, and it is desirable to control it. Trees should be thinned to improve ventilation and sunshine penetration.

Algae and mosses.

Lichens on an olive tree. (LEONARDO SCHENA)

Lichens on an olive tree.

Lichens and mosses.

Dryness in a mature tree is a sign that branches are dying.

Parasitic plants

Mistletoe

Viscum album var. *album (L.)* [Loranthaceae] and *V. cruciatum (Sieb)* [Santalaceae]

Mistletoes are a group of evergreen hemi-parasitic plants that parasitise the stems of olive trees. They attach themselves to a tree, draining nutrients from the host, but they are not totally dependent on it. Leaves of the mistletoe contain chlorophyll and are capable of making their own food from carbon dioxide and water like other plants. Birds feed on the mistletoe berries and transfer seeds to new hosts via their droppings. When a seed germinates, it grows through the bark and into the vascular system of the host, where it obtains water and minerals.

Mistletoe on an olive tree.

Lenticels

Lenticels can be seen on fruit surfaces, and also on the stems/bark and roots. Olive leaves have stomata on their underside (abassial) surfaces only. Stomata are nestled in peltate trichomes that restrict water loss and make the olive relatively resistant to drought. Both stomata and lenticels are involved in gas exchange. Both allow the release of water vapour into the atmosphere.

Below left: Small brown corky growths up to 2–5 mm wide that form on the surface of stems from enlarged lenticels (breathing holes in bark). These cells can rupture from the high water pressure, with stains of black sooty mould associated with sap.

Below right: Lenticels on olive fruits can respond to disease development.

CHAPTER 4

Management

Pests, diseases and disorders are almost always the result of plant stress. These include: nutrient deficiency, water stress, temperature extremes and chemical damage. Pest infestations often coincide with climatic changes such as irregular rainfall, increased humidity or drought. Pest outbreaks may have a devastating impact in a given year, but cause only marginal losses in other years.

Of course, not all pests and diseases of olive trees have a high incidence, making it possible to live with some of them. When olive pests are identified early and the appropriate treatments applied, pests can be easily controlled. In nature there are natural predators that maintain balance and help us keep harmful insects under control. Even so, under certain conditions it will be necessary to apply specific control treatments.

What do we want to know about the disease or pest that would help us to control it?

What are the most important steps to improve disease or pest control?

A disease is a condition in a plant that affects the plant's normal functioning or development. For a disease or pest to occur, three conditions must be met.

1. A pathogen has to be present on or in the plant.
2. There need to be suitable environmental conditions for the pathogen.
3. The plant must be susceptible to the disease.

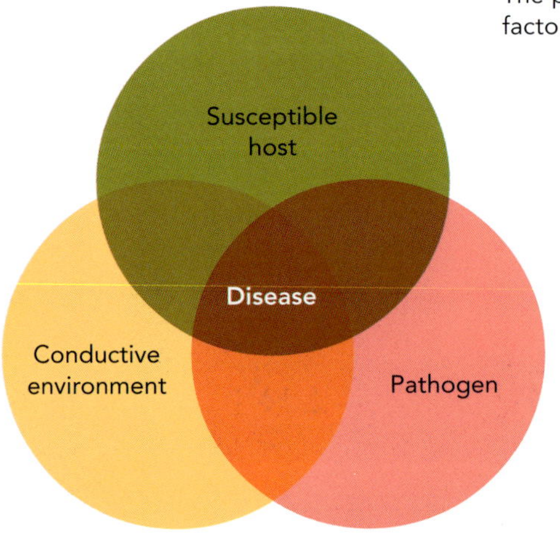

The plant-disease triangle represents the factors necessary for disease to occur.

What is IPDM?

Due to the growth in the industry it has become even more important to address the issues of product quality and the adoption of **Integrated Pest and Disease Management (IPDM)**.

IPDM is the integration of approaches and methods into a pest-management system that takes into consideration the ecology of the disease(s) or pest(s) and trees. IPDM is a common-sense approach to minimising crop damage by pests and diseases. It uses a number of simultaneously applied control methods which, collectively, discourage pests or diseases and encourage beneficial organisms, leading to a more balanced crop ecosystem that gives improved quality produce with minimal adverse effects on the environment.

Grove design and olive cultivar selection

Establishing a healthy, productive olive grove requires planning and preparation.

These factors will help to determine potential grove productivity:

- Consider tree-planting density (low density, high density, super-high density) and canopy architecture, proposed harvest method, frost control, soil moisture management (berms and drainage channels), wind breaks and staking of young trees.
- Consider olive-cultivar selection, including verification of DNA status, regional environment, agronomic (pollination, tree vigour, precocity, alternate bearing), pest and disease resistance, frost tolerance, market attributes (for olive oil: oil content, extraction efficiency, flavour profile and oxidative stability; for table olives: flesh, stone ratio, fruit size and flesh quality (resistance to bruising, sensory profile for the intended processing method).

Things to consider for successfully growing olives:

1. *Is the land suitable for growing olives commercially?*

- Climate – specifically the microclimates on the property.
- Soil – type and fertility.
- Well drained soils and consider the aspect.
- Is it possible to provide adequate irrigation.

2. *Variety selection*

- Use only cultivars that are suitable for the climate, soil type, pests and diseases in your area.
- Select varieties suitable for the market you would like to target – oil, table olives, leaves.

3. *Source of trees*

- Choose a highly regarded nursery specialising in olive trees.
- Ensure your selected varieties are available.
- Ensure no disease exist on the nursery stock.

4. *Planting*

- Effect of other trees in or near a grove.
- Proper ground preparation.
- Set up irrigation.
- Tree spacing and row direction.

5. *Caring for olive trees*

'A healthy tree is a strong and disease-resistant tree.'

- What is a healthy tree?
- Is the ecosystem balanced?
- Prevention is better than cure.
- A physically, nutritionally and biologically balanced soil is the most productive and stable.

6. *Dealing with pests, diseases and disorders*

- Correct identification – is it a pest, disease or disorder?
- Monitoring.
- What treatments are available and appropriate?
- Biological versus Chemical solutions.
- Ensure you do not destroy grove's biosystem.

7. *Factors affect the farmer's choice of pesticide – to spray or not to spray?*

- Approval for the intended use – crop and pest.
- Pesticide efficacy (does it kill the pest?).
- Safety for the environment.
- Safety for beneficial species.
- Safety for yourself and for other people and their property.
- Price.
- Easy of use.
- Avoiding resistance.
- Ability to stimulate pests and diseases.
- Incomplete or missing information.
- Pesticides can cause stress to the plants they were intended to defend.
- Complete coverage of large, tall trees is hard to achieve; spraying is not very efficient and might not be justified or feasible.
- Application of chemical treatments is difficult in rainy years.
- Pesticide residues can persist until the harvest stage, risking possible contamination of fruits.

Monitoring

The most important part of any pest and disease management system is monitoring. Regular monitoring, with effective recording of the results, provides important information that helps in making decisions on whether and when action should be taken, and how effective actions have been.

Use a magnifying lens to inspect samples of leaves, twigs, flowers and fruit for the presence of pests, diseases or damage and their stages of development. Assessing individual trees is important for early detection of pests and diseases. If a pest or disease is detected, check surrounding trees in the row and in adjacent rows to establish the extent of the infestation.

Monitoring can be done with simple visual inspections, but normally traps are used for capturing pest individuals or fungal spores. Pest monitoring using pheromones is key to determining the presence of some olive pests (such as olive fruit fly and olive moth) and their flight seasons, establishing the population levels and deciding the correct timing for phytosanitary treatments, which should always be done with authorised products in accordance with current legislation and in a rational way. Monitoring after an intervention, such as pesticide application, will demonstrate its level of success.

The Modern Approach To Pest and Disease Control – IPDM

Soil organisms, including bacteria, fungi, protozoans, nematodes, mites, springtails and earthworms, perform a vast array of fertility-maintenance tasks. Organic soil management aims at helping soil organisms to maintain fertility. Conventional (non-organic) soil management merely substitutes a simplified chemical system to provide nutrients to plants. Once a healthy soil ecosystem is disrupted by the excessive use of soluble synthetic fertilisers, restoring it can be a long and costly process. In many cases, the excessive use of energy-intensive petroleum-based fertilisers and pesticides has destroyed the biological fertility of soil, so growers use ever-larger amounts of these materials to sustain crop growth.

Soil management and Regenerative farming

The importance of regenerative farming for olives

Research shows that the ability of a crop plant to resist or tolerate insect pests and diseases is tied to optimal physical, chemical and mainly biological properties of soils. Soils with high organic matter and active soil biology generally exhibit good soil fertility.

Chemically treated soils produce weaker plants that are more physiologically stressed and these plants become more susceptible to disease and insect damage as well. Therefore olive growers should use chemicals wisely and only where necessary and focus more on enhancing tree health and vigour. Healthy, productive plants can use their natural defence systems to resist environmental stresses. As a result, they need less chemical input for survival and productive long-term growth. Pests can be present without causing economic damage. Soils support the growth of tree life. They are a crucial element of land-based ecosystems and oleiculture.

Good practices are about a creating harmony with nature that starts with soil and builds resilience from the ground up. In many ways, it's about bringing olive groves back to a state that existed before the mass industrialisation of agriculture. Or, simply, it's about replicating nature in the groves. Nature is full of diversity, but conventional farming strips that back.

Wallaby with an olive branch in an olive grove. Olives connect agriculture, farmers and biodiversity.

A living soil

The living part of the soil is just as critical to plant growth as the physical soil structures.

Soil microorganisms are the essential link between mineral reserves and plant growth. The cycles that permit nutrients to flow from soil to plant are all interdependent and they work only with the help of the living organisms that constitute the soil community.

Like all living things, the creatures of the soil community need food, water and air to carry on their activities. The provision of plenty of organic material, enough moisture and well-aerated soil will keep their populations thriving.

Farm-management practices are focused on improving soil health through applying biological methods, such as compost, biochar, creating biofertilisers, extensive mulching and cover cropping. These practices also help to increase the water-holding capacity of the soil and to minimise evaporation, which will become increasingly important as climate change takes hold.

Providing plants with the proper nutrition will help to keep them in optimum health, and enable them to fight off attacks from diseases and pests. 'Feed the soil, not the plant' is a concept fundamental to organic soil management. When the ecosystem thrives, so do the trees and we produce amazing olive oil.

As public interest in sustainability continues to increase and broaden in scope, the demand for rigorous, meaningful assurances of responsible farming and processing practices has grown.

Building on its successful family of leading labels, A Greener World's Certified Regenerative program is a whole-farm, plan-based regenerative certification, giving farmers, consumers, and buyers confidence in terms of reliability and impact.

Olive pruning material chipped and spread on the ground.

Soil management with permanent natural green cover.

Compost near an olive grove.

Soil management with mulching. (ROGER HARRISON)

Soil management with permanent natural green cover.

Mechanical management of green cover.

Management of pruning material

Agronomic practices commonly used in olive growing include annual or biennial pruning operations. Generally, the resulting wood residues are burnt on site or taken away. Some farmers chose to chip the residues to be scattered on the ground or buried.

The advantage of chopped pruned material is its mulching effect, reducing water loss and soil erosion, increasing the soil's organic-matter content, improving soil structure and reducing weed growth.

Olive-mill pomace application in olive groves

Use of composted olive-mill pomace as an organic amendment in olive groves should be considered as a viable option for the safe disposal of the main waste of the olive-oil industry and for the restoration of frequently degraded olive-grove soils.

Weed control

Traditional weed control typically involves either the physical removal of the weeds or the use of herbicides.

Herbicides. Total reliance on herbicides has several other disadvantages in addition to the obvious impact on the environment.

Grazing. Sheep eat almost all weeds down to ground level, which reduces weed competition, but does not eliminate it. Goats are browsers, so they must be carefully managed to protect the trees.

Cover crops are planted in some groves to replace the resident weed vegetation on the orchard floor. Cover crops can be planted between the tree rows, and in the spring a 'mow-and-throw' mower can be used to cut the cover crops and throw them in the tree rows.

Mulching. Applying a layer of mulch around the tree's base can help suppress weed growth, conserve moisture, enhance the visual appeal of the tree's surroundings and create better conditions for root growth.

Sheep graze the grass between rows of olive trees, reducing fire risk and controlling weeds.

Resistant varieties and their role in disease management

Resistant varieties are an important cultural disease management practice to include in a disease management program.

Since many olive cultivars are self-sterile or nearly so, they are generally planted in pairs with a single primary cultivar and a secondary cultivar selected for its ability to fertilise the primary one. In recent times, efforts have been directed at producing hybrid cultivars with qualities useful to farmers, such as resistance to disease, quick growth and larger or more consistent crops.

New types of olive trees have been created over the years, both by adaptation to different climates and multiplication methods. Varieties have been bred with resistance to many, but unfortunately not all, important diseases caused by different types of pathogens, including fungi, bacteria, viruses, nematodes and so on. Today there are more than 2,000 varieties of olives grown worldwide.

Cultivar 'Koroneki'.

Cultivar 'Frantoio'.

The white olive variety 'Leucocarpa', or 'Leucolea'.

Cultivar 'Zarza'.

Cultivar 'Arbequina'.

Cultivar 'Vera'.

Cultivar 'Manzanillo'.

Cultivar 'Arbosana'.

Cultivar 'Nevadillo Blanco'.

Cultivar 'Barnea'.

The plant cell wall serves a variety of functions:

Circulates and distributes water, minerals and other nutrients.

Regulates growth and protects the plant from diseases and pests (plants do not have an immune system so the cell wall is a good barrier).

Cell-wall thickness may influence resistance to certain pathogens.

Influence of location and importance of varieties

An olive variety of Italian, Spanish, Greek or Israeli origin will not necessarily behave in the same manner in respect to quality or quantity of olives if grown somewhere else in the world. Location has influenced many of the Old World varieties when brought into the New World. The selection of olive varieties for a grove is very important.

Each cultivar has specific genetic characteristics that determine its susceptibility or resistance to pests and diseases, soil conditions and climate. These factors, including resistance to frost and drought, should be considered when choosing varieties for an olive grove. Different olive cultivars have varying responses to flower and fruit infection.

Olive varieties have fruits with different colours. The colour of an olive is an indication of its ripeness. Green olives ripen and become anything from light brown, to vibrant red or purple, to the deepest, darkest black.

White olives reportedly taste sweeter than commercially produced green and black olives as they have comparatively lower levels of bitter-tasting antioxidants. The oil produced by white olives is similar to that of black and green olives, except that it has a shorter shelf life.

Disease resistance and adaptability of olive cultivars

Assessing the susceptibility of olive cultivars:

Anthracnose

- Highly susceptible: Kalamata, Cornicabra, Lechín de Sevilla, Manzanilla de Sevilla, Morona, Ocal, Picudo, Verdial de Huevar, Jumbo Kalmata, Hojiblanca, Galega Vulgar, Galega Cobrançosa, UC13A6, Barnea, Chiquitita, UC-I 2-68, UC-I 8-20, UC-I1311-10, Sevillano, Manzanillo and Hojiblanca.
- Susceptible: Arbosana, Arbequina, Morrut, Pajarero and Villalonga.
- Resistant: Blanqueta, Empeltre, Morona-D, Razzola, Frantoio, Koroneiki, Leccino, Morona-D, Picual, Frantoio, Coratina and Correggiola.

Note. In warm and humid parts of Australia, Barnea is much more susceptible to anthracnose during the growing season compared to plants of the same variety grown in Israel, which has a hot, dry climate.

The olive variety Lazzero adapts well to multiple climatic environments and has high resistance to diseases.

Peacock spot

- Highly susceptible: Blanqueta, Callosina, Cornicabra, Empeltre, Lechin de Granada, Manzanilla de Sevilla, Meski, Morisca, Ocal, Pajarero, Picholine Marroquí, Verdial de Huevar, Verdial de Velez-Malaga, Hojiblanca and Picual.
- Moderately susceptible: Alameno de Cabra, Changlot Real, Gordal Sevillana, Lucio, Morona, Manzanilla del Piquito, Alfafara, Bical, Cobrançosa, Manzanilla Cacereña, Morrut, Picudo and Arbequina.
- Resistant: Chetoui, Frantoio, Megaritiki, Racimal, Rapasayo, Koroneiki, Leccino, Picholine and Sevillano.
- Highly resistant: Arbosana, Cipressino, Dolce Agogia, Galega Vulgar, Oblonga, Lechín de Sevilla and Manzanilla de Montefrío.

Cercosporiose

- Susceptible: Correggiola, Moraiolo, Moresca, Rosciola and Ogliarola.
- Moderetely susceptible: Coratina, Hojiblanca, Leccino, Arbequina, Manzanilla de Sevilla, Picual, Picudo, Frantoio and Coratina.
- Resistant: Tonda Iblea and Nocellara Etnea.

Verticillium wilt incited by the defoliating pathotype (*Verticillium dahlia*)

- Highly susceptible: Arbequina, Ayvalik, Borriolenca, Bouteillan, Callosina, Carrasqueno de Lucena, Chemlal de Kabilye, Dulzal de Carmona Fulla de Salce, Gordal de Hellin, Imperial de Jaen, Manzanilla, Manzanilla Cacerena, Megaritiki, Morona, Nabali, Pendolino Negro del Carpio, Nevadillo Blanco de Jaen, Picual, Amfissis, Mastoidis and Hojiblanca.
- Susceptible: Arbosana, Ascolana Tenera, Azapa, Dokkar, Kalogerida, Zarza, Souri, Nabali, Manzanillo and Barnea.
- Moderately susceptible: Cipresino, Koroneiki, Oblonga, Sevillenca, Tragolia and Atsiholou.
- Resistant: Changlot Real, Empeltre, Frantoio and Leccino.

Cold damage

- Susceptible: Empeltre, Moraiolo, Taggiasca, Barnea, Frantoio, Manzanillo and Nevadillo.
- Moderately susceptible: Kalamon, Picholine, Sevillano, Arbequina, Azapa, Kalamata, Picual, Salome, Verdale and Koroneiki.
- Resistant: Aglandau, Ascolano, Barouni, Bosana, Bouteillan, Chemlali, Coratina, Cornicabra, Farga, Hojiblanca, Leccino, Maurino, Mission, Pendolino, Picudo, Picholine, Sevillano, Volos, Lazzero and Correggiola.

Drought damage

- Highly susceptible: Ocal, Blanquette, Madural, Coratina Sevillenca, Sevillano, Kalamata, Moraiolo, Vernina, and Frantoio are the most drought-sensitive varieties.
- Susceptible: Arbequina and Grappuda.
- Resistant: Leccino, Morisca, Verdial, Cornicobra, Americano, Piangente and Amellau.
- Highly resistant: Picholine Marocaine, Lechin de Sevilla, Azeradj, Koroneiki and Hojiblanca.

Salinity

- Sensitive: Chalkidikis, Throubolia, Aguromanaki, Leccino, Bouteillan, Nabal, Pajarero, Chetoui, Calego, Cobrancosa and Meski.
- Moderately tolerant: Amphissis, Koroneiki, Mastoidis, Valanolia, Adramitini, Maurino, Coratina, Carolea, Moraiolo, Olia Manna, Manzanillo, Aggezi, Toffahi, Nabali and Muhassan.
- Tolerant: Megaritiki, Lianolia Kerkiras, Kalamata, Kothreiki, Frantoio, Arbequina, Picual, Jabaluna Nevadillo, Lechin de Sivilla, Cañivano, Esscarabajuelo, Hamed and Chemlali.

Plant propagation and nursery management

Olive trees host a number of diseases caused by fungi, bacteria, phytoplasmas, viruses and other agents of diseases of unknown etiology. These disseminate by propagating material and are the subject of certification programs in many countries.

> The use of healthy planting stock is critical to the biosecurity and resilience of olive trees. To avoid disease dissemination through vegetative propagation, possible remedies include mainly preventive strategies based on the use and propagation of healthy parent plants.

Nurseries are a very important component of the olive sector in terms of the multiplication and certification of planting materials. The main techniques which are now used commercially for olive propagation are rooting of cuttings and grafting of seedlings. The prevalence of one depends on many factors, including the genotype to be propagated, the production area, agronomic needs, traditions and the market. In any case, the nursery chain is focused on the production of higher-quality plants, which helps to prevent the spread of quarantine diseases, and on traceability implemented by the certification of the propagation.

No matter which way a tree is started, you're sure to get a higher survival rate by picking healthy trees grown in a nursery.

Regardless of the propagation system, the best plants are those of one to one-and-a-half years in age (in the case of grafted plants, from the moment of grafting), with a minimum height greater than 80–100cm (32–40in), grown in pots with a volume of about 4 litres (8.5 pints), with a well-developed root system.

Olive-tree seedlings can be propagated by different methods of asexual propagation, such as micropropagation, microcutting and minicutting. Their complete development takes place in no-soil cultivation systems, involving aseptic culture of small portions of tissues or plant organs, on artificial nutrient substrates, inside containers and in controlled environmental conditions, producing high-quality disease-free plants.

Inside the vessels, the plants are grown on culture media that contain nutrients and growth regulators, and are described as *in vitro*, which means 'in glass'. In contrast, soil-grown plants are described as *in vivo*. Plants that are propagated *in vitro* are smaller than *in vivo* plants, hence the term 'micropropagation'. Because of the high costs involved, micropropagation in olives has not yet replaced the traditional propagation systems such as rooted cuttings and grafting.

Left: Micropropogation, olive explants established in an *in vitro* crop. Somatic embryo germination and root development. Regenerated plantlet. (KHAYREDDINE TITOUH)

Centre: Propagating olive trees from seeds. Right: Propagating from cuttings at an olive nursery.

Nutrients in plant health and pest management

- Proper nutrition can stimulate the production of physical and chemical defences to cope with pathogens, which improve plant resistance.
- A healthy photosynthetic capacity also allows for a quick growth response to a pathogen invasion.

Thus healthy plants can better tolerate increased disease burdens than plants stressed by nutrient deficiency.

Nutrients can reduce pests and diseases to an acceptable level that permits further control, if needed, by other cultural practices or conventional organic biocides, which are more successful and less expensive.

Olive nutritional status and tolerance to biotic and abiotic stresses

Although plant tolerance to pests and disease is a genetic characteristic, it can also be affected by environmental factors such as plant nutrition. The effect depends on the nutrient, plant species and parasite, although it may be small in very tolerant or very susceptible cultivars.

Overall, excess Nitrogen (N) tends to favour disease development, while Potassium (K) deficiency increases susceptibility to parasites. The efficiency of disease control also depends on the N:K ratio, since the effect of K may vary depending on the plant's N nutritional status.

Nitrogen (N). Excessive nitrogen fertilisation encourages the development of scale insects, psyllids, olive peacock spot, anthracnose diseases and soil fungus. Excess nitrogen accumulates in the fruit, and negatively affects fruit quality. A management practice that recommends nitrogen application only when the previous season's leaf analysis indicates that nitrogen has dropped below deficiency level will optimise nitrogen fertilisation and promote environmentally responsible use of nitrogen fertilisers.

In the Northern Hemisphere in October, before the onset of dormancy, excess N resulted in increased frost tolerance. During dormancy, all the trees exhibited greater tolerance to low temperatures. In spring, after budbreak, trees become more sensitive and with an excess of N they were more sensitive to low temperatures.

Magnesium (Mg) is essential to plant development; it is required by plants to produce chlorophyll (magnesium is part of the chlorophyll in all green plants and essential for photosynthesis) and helps the tree resist olive lace bug attack. Magnesium also helps plants to absorb phosphorous, increases a plant's natural resistance to disease and is absorbed by both the leaves and the roots.

Boron (B) is the most important trace element for olive trees. Foliar sprayings with boron during the formation of new vegetation and at the beginning of blossoming also have positive outcomes. Boron is essential to increase fruit set. It is usually applied before flowering and after fruit set through foliar applications.

Potassium (K) plays an important role in the regulation of water status in the olive, improving drought tolerance. It is well known that K-deficient plants lose water more easily than well-nourished ones. Under drought stress conditions, K regulates stomatal opening and helps plants adapt to water deficits.

For a relatively salt-tolerant and economically important crop, applications of K and Ca are recommended in order to mitigate the harmful effects of salinity and to develop agriculture in, for instance, coastal saline land. K fertilisation is recommended to reduce frost damage in the spring.

Calcium (Ca) reduces fruit drop, accelerates flower opening, promotes fruit quality, makes stronger cell walls and plays a role in the regulation of the stomata. It might also promote metabolic processes leading to effective uptake of other nutrients and minerals.

Calcium nitrate has an alkaline reaction and would be suitable for applications where soil pH is acidic or near neutral. Calcium is involved in the sodium-exclusion mechanism, which can increase tolerance to salinity. Oyster shell lime is used to raise pH in acidic soils in Japan. Finely ground oyster shells contain up to 39 per cent calcium plus a natural balance of other nutrients and micronutrients.

Lime sulphur inhibits the germination of spores and affects the growth of fungi. How it works on mites and insects remains unclear. Pesticides with calcium sulphide or calcium polysulphide as the active ingredient are used as fungicides, insecticides and acaricides.

Silicon (Si) is not an essential element for plant growth, but it is considered a beneficial element; among its roles in the control of pests and diseases is the formation of a physical barrier that occurs through silicon deposition in the epidermal cells of the leaves. The presence of soluble silicon also facilitates the deposition of phenolic and other compounds at sites of infection, which is a general defence mechanism to pathogen attack. In olives, silicon application, either by foliar sprays or through irrigation water, reduces the incidence of olive peacock spot.

Irrigation management

Influence of irrigation on insect and disease control

The olive tree is a typical dry-soil plant which, when grown under dry-farming conditions, uses natural rainfall accumulated in the soil and is not usually given additional water to offset the effects of long periods of water deficit.

In general terms, supplementary irrigation should be adapted to the year's climatic variations and the tree's status to ensure minimum water stressing during the period from flowering to fruit maturity and to avoid decreasing the tree's activity when it is mostly needed.

Irrigation does not influence fruit shape, but increases its weight, volume and flesh/pit ratio. The water content in the flesh of irrigated olive fruits will increase and the firmness might be slightly less than in rain-fed olives which lack water during their cell enlargement.

Also, since phenols are water-soluble and since the amount of vegetation water produced during oil extraction of dry-farmed olives is less, the oil will consequently retain slightly higher phenols which would have been lost in the higher moisture content.

Irrigation of olive tree makes it possible to:

- Protect against the risk of drought with the possibility of excellent yields materialising.
- Counteract alternate bearing cycles, thus allowing the trees to produce simultaneously both the fruit and the branches (vegetation) that will bear the fruit the following year.
- Improve production in terms of quantity and quality; in particular by allowing the tree to produce a maximum of perfect flowers and ensure their setting.
- Allow fertilisers, diluted into the irrigation water and applied very precisely, to be made available to the olive tree, directly into the root zone.

- Accelerate the growth of young olive plants.
- Regulate fruit moisture which impacts on yields and processing efficiency. Excessive fruit moisture becomes an issue for oil extraction and whenever possible it should be maintained through proper irrigation scheduling.
- Lack of water at an early stage followed by a sudden growth spurt can cause the skin on olive fruits to split and for them to fall off the tree. This is as a result of variations in the water supply available at the roots. Rot may subsequently take hold.
- The rational use of irrigation water management and irrigation networks in combination with adequate ground management are very important for management of the olive fly, anthracnose and root rot diseases (overwatering should be avoided).

The numerous olive growing districts are characterised by deep differences in climate and soil and in the frequency and nature of environmental stress.

Olive groves around the world:

Clockwise from top left: Argentina. (VI INT. SYMP. OLIVE GROWING 2012); Egypt. (MOHAMED EL-KHOLY); Spain. (ANTONIO TRAPERO); Peru. (JOHN SYMINGTON); Australia. (JAMES FARLEY); South Africa.

Canopy Management

Influence of pruning on insect and disease control

Keep trees properly maintained through pruning helps with natural disease control and reduces pressure on pesticides. Proper pruning and trimming techniques play a vital role in maintaining the health and longevity of trees. When done correctly, pruning promotes tree growth, improves structure, enhances aesthetics and reduces the risk of disease and damage.

Regular trimming of smaller branches can also help maintain a desirable shape and prevent branches from rubbing against each other. Proper pruning not only keeps trees healthy but also improves their overall appearance, ensures safety, and allows for better air circulation and light penetration.

Olive trees need some pruning every two to three years. The objectives of pruning are to encourage new growth, prune out suckers and any cankered or dead twigs, remove and destroy fruit mummies when pruning to reduce initial fungal inoculum, open the olive tree up to improve airflow to help control pest and diseases and to allow fruit to ripen on the inside as well as at the edges of the tree, remove unproductive branches and reduce canopy size.

Jagged cuts left by mechanical pruning should be removed by hand pruning, leaving a neat cut to avoid infection and die back.

Fresh cuts made while pruning are made doubly vulnerable to infection by fungal and bacterial pathogens if done in the rain, with the cut being an ideal entry point for pathogens.

Pruning should be avoided if hard frosts are likely.

Heavy pruning of olive trees can lead to increased reflected light, while radiated heat around trees can lead to sunburn. Encourage branch structure with proper pruning. Retain branches that will help to shade the trunk and be beneficial for cropping.

Pruning during late autumn or winter or is generally recommended in order to minimise stress on the tree.

Maintenance of pruning equipment decreases the likelihood of infection – disinfection is recommended.

Management of Suckers and Watersprouts

Olive trees produce basitonic shoots (suckers), which they send out from the base of the trunk. Suckers are horizontal new growth. If suckers grow higher on the trunk, they're called watersprouts and they usually occur at the site of a pruning wound, a crack or some other damage.

Suckers are a tree's attempt to grow more branches, often in response to some kind of injury or overpruning.

- One of the biggest management challenges from post-fire regrowth is the proliferation of suckers around the base of trunks.

Lace bug infection.

Anthracnose disease.

Suckers and watersprouts grow after heavy pruning.

- Olive suckers and watersprouts harbour pests and diseases and should always be removed while they are still young.
- Suckers shooting from rootstock can cause significant and costly losses in olive crops, competing for nutrients and water and reducing potential fruit production.
- They also physically interfere with mechanical olive harvesting, which requires a straight clear trunk for 1–1.2m (3–4ft) from the ground. This section needs to be free from branches to allow the harvester to grip the trunk without obstruction and to reduce damage to the tree.

The use of herbicides to destroy the suckers is not recommended. An application of any herbicide (contact or systemic) to the suckers is likely to damage or kill the tree.

Regular pruning of suckers as they appear throughout the growing season is the best way to keep them well managed.

Pruning paint.

Whitewashing/lime paint on olive trees.

Wound-sealing pastes/paint

After any pruning or cutting it is advisable to cover the wounds with wound-sealing pastes or paint and to spray the trees with a copper-based fungicide, in order to prevent the tree from developing bacterial or fungal infections.

Painting tree trunks with lime

Painted onto tree trunks, limewash prevents disease, sunburn or frost injury. To put it simply, limewashing a tree helps sanitise it and protects it from the proliferation of parasites and diseases to rid the trunk of pest eggs and fungal spores. Lime wash acts as a physical barrier, making the tree trunk less attractive to insects and pests. Tree whitening regulates temperature fluctuations. The expansion lichens and mosses is limited by tree whitening.

Lather lime paint onto tree trunks, from the ground to the base of primary branches. Bark should be perfectly dry before application.

Warning: Lime may worsen tree wounds because lime milk can penetrate tissues.

Kaolin clay – barrier film and barrier film sprays

Kaolin is mixed with water and used as a physical repellent. Preventive kaolin sprays with milk and sulphur solution should good results. The kaolin barrier created by the particle film protects the treated plant surfaces from diseases and insects and also protects the plants from environmental stresses.

Kaolin application.

Fire management

Although a fire-affected olive grove can look devastated, trees could have the potential to recover and be productive again if managed well.

Assessment and recovery

Assess groves based on the extent of the damage. A low-intensity fire does not kill larger olive trees with trunks and branches larger than 20mm (0.8in) in diameter; but younger trees with stems smaller than this can die.

Tree recovery depends on:

- Degree of heat damage.
- Tree size and age.
- Moisture stress before and after the event.
- The presence of undamaged trunks and scaffold branches above any graft unions.

If cuttings were planted, all regrowth can be used to retrain a new tree. Olive trees can begin resprouting within just a couple of weeks.

Recovery of olives after fire is likely to involve:

- Pruning.
- Replacement or repair of the irrigation system.
- Some nutrition management.
- Patience while the trees reshoot and indicate the percentage of recovery.

For pruning, decisions should take into account the following:

- Severity of damage and losses.
- Tree age.
- Olive variety.
- Rootstock.
- Planting densities.

Irrigation will assist the speed at which full production can be achieved, although volumes applied may need to be less.

During the recovery period, trees undergoing simulated post-fire regrowth have lower moisture stress and higher soil moisture availability than intact trees with full canopies. Recovering trees only need half as much water because of the presence of a smaller leaf area per root zone volume.

Fertiliser will be less important than irrigation. Olive trees don't require large amounts of fertiliser.

Because of the small leaf area of the recovering trees in relation to large root mass, regrowth should be rapid and vigorous and extra applications of nutrients may make the task of reshaping the trees more problematic. It could also delay the return to fruiting because of excessive vigour.

Frost management

Reducing the risk

Frost fans are an increasingly common tool in very large groves and vineyards but for smaller growers they're not always affordable.

Moving air or drift

Moving air or drift reduces the freezing ability of surface water – for example, heavy dew – on small parts of plants such as flower buds.

Pruning trees well and keeping a gap of at least 1m (3.3ft) between the canopy and the ground helps to encourage the natural drift of air across the grove, reducing the freezing effect of the frost.

Optimise tree health

Lots of leaves on a tree – and healthy leaves – can also help protect the tree. Every plant cell is giving off a tiny amount of heat and if it's healthy that can prevent flower buds being burned due to frost.

As with any other major stress, a healthy tree can always survive better through a frost.

Winter irrigation

Ground water in the middle of winter can be 14–15°C (57–59°F), so applying 3–4l (5–7 pints) per dripper under olive trees during frost conditions of 0°C (32°F) or below adds latent heat to the ground and helps to keep the temperature higher.

Fog can also provide frost protection as the dew point helps to buffer frost.

Soil biology

Increasing the biological content in the soil under olive trees and increasing the carbon content in the soil will increase the soil temperature.

Additional grove management practices to avoid frost include:

- Mowing high grass adds 1°C (1.8°F).
- Bare soil allows the sun to heat it up. Moist soil will store heat from sunlight better than dry soil. Keeping soil bare and moist can add 1°C (1.8°F).
- Water over trees can also assist, as the temperature of the water adds heat and wet ice around fruit prevents the temperature of the fruit itself falling below 0°C (32°F).

Further advice on planning and monitoring:

- Identifying frost risk areas on your property – both before you plant and when considering mitigation measures – is a no-brainer.
- Choice and positioning of varieties. Some varieties are less frost sensitive and early ripening varieties should be planted in higher risk areas: frost monitoring is also crucial, due to the need to identify affected fruit and harvest and process it immediately in order to protect oil quality.

Integrating solar energy into olive groves

Solar panels installed between olive trees provide energy to power water pumping and irrigation – this protects fruit from extreme weather events and improves water efficiency.

Wind management

Even though olives grow into large trees, they still benefit from some wind protection, especially when they are young. This reduces the chance of bruising on the fruit and reduces the drying effects of wind over the summer period. Trees need shelter to prevent wind damage to the lush canopy and fruit, and against wind-generated soil erosion. Shelter should be established several years in advance of planting the olives. This is because, like the young of all species, olives are much more vulnerable to wind damage during their establishment phase. Most growers rely on natural tree shelters. It is important to select species that are adapted to the local conditions.

Stone walls and stones around olive trees as protective windbreaks on the French island of Corsica. (FABIENNE MAESTRACCI)

Windbreaks in New Zealand. Wind damage can be avoided in windy areas through the use of living windbreaks such as cypress and eucalyptus.

Windbreaks (Shelterbelts)

Windbreaks, or shelterbelts, are plantings of single or multiple rows of wind-tolerant trees or shrubs. In some countries with extreme climatic conditions, windbreaks are an essential part of property management. Windbreaks reduce wind speed, filtering and breaking the force of the wind, providing protection from hot and cold winds.

Windbreaks can reduce windspeeds and windchill. They also enhance soil fertility, mitigate the effects of soil erosion and secondary salinity, increase water infiltration and store large amounts of carbon.

The art of dry stone walling is practised in countries such as Croatia, Cyprus, France, Greece, Italy and Spain. Positioning these walls around an olive grove protect the olive trees from the impact of the bora (a cold, dry wind that blows from the north – a phenomenon which occurs when the wind from the turbulent sea lifts drops of seawater and creates 'sea smoke').

Shelterbelts provide many benefits to farms, including:

- Protection of crops, livestock and homes.
- Reduction of soil erosion.
- Salinity control.
- Improved biodiversity.

Mammal management

In areas where attacks from mammals such as rodents and rabbits may occur, it is advisable to apply tube-shaped guards to the plants, made from rigid plastic pipes (generally polypropylene). These guards also facilitate soil management operations along the rows, reducing the risk of damaging the plants with mechanical tools and avoiding the risk of herbicides coming into direct contact with the olive plants.

There are various techniques to scare away and repel wild animals:

- Use of perfumes, strange smells and danger indicators.
- Tools to make noises.
- Placement of electric fences or fences.
- Use of commercial repellents.
- Sacks, ribbons or bottles hanging.
- Homemade repellents.

Animals usually end up getting used to noises and smells.

A bark trunk protector can prevent damage by rabbits and other animals.

Pest and Disease Management

Pests and diseases are present in olive groves year-round, making very difficult to control them. Many plant pathogenic fungi spend the winter in a dormant state, usually on old plant material or in the soil. They create special survival structures with dark pigmentation and thick walls to help them survive extended cold and dry periods.

To avoid exposure to severe cold and or fluctuating temperatures, many insects overwinter in protected areas, sheltered from the extremes, often under plant debris or burrowed into the soil. The reason temperature has little effect on their survival is related to their lifecycle. Depending on the species, insects overwinter in all life stages, including adults, eggs, larvae and chrysalises or cocoons.

While scientific advances in the field of olive research are encouraging, olive agriculture in some regions currently faces significant challenges which threaten its very existence. It is difficult to control pests and pathogens, but olive cultivation is under scrutiny to utilise more nature-positive crop-management methods.

These challenges not only affect the agricultural sector, but also link to other economic branches such as the culinary tourism or oleotourism, an emerging concept that is starting to gain importance in regions heavily invested in olive agriculture.

Why is natural control preferable to chemical control?

Although pesticides are often used to protect olive crops against pests and disease attacks, there is increasing concern about the effects of pesticides on the environment, human health and product quality.

Unfortunately, continuous use of chemicals is not just expensive, it leads to pesticide resistance, residues on olives and loss of biodiversity. Pesticides do not solve the pest problem. In the past 50 years, pesticide use has increased tenfold, while crop losses from pest damage have doubled. Chemically treated soils produce weaker plants that are more physiologically stressed, and these plants become more susceptible to disease and insect damage as well.

Biological and non-chemical plant protection is increasingly important worldwide as an alternative to the use of conventional chemical pesticides.

Insecticides should be used only when pest populations are not longer under the adequate control of natural and biological control agents.

Biological and biotechnical methods for olive pest control

The use of biological control methods can reduce spraying costs and lead to a reduction in the potential for pesticide resistance. Biological control involves the mass-production and release of natural enemies such as parasitoids and predators to control pest insects in an environmentally sound manner.

Olive growers say: "Naturally it is organically grown – better for us as the growers, better for the environment and above all, better for you."

Biological control

Biological control is the use of natural enemies (parasites, predators or pathogens) of pests. The natural enemies are also called 'beneficial organisms' or 'beneficials'. The aim of biological control is to establish and maintain populations of beneficial organisms which will keep pest populations below economically damaging levels.

There are two main groups of beneficial insects:

- Predators – attack and eat other insects. Either adult or larvae, or both may be predatory.
- Parasites – lay eggs on or in other insects. The eggs hatch and the developing larvae consume the host, usually from the inside.

Natural enemies may be mass-reared and released into orchards. Augmentative releases aim to ensure that the natural enemy is present in sufficient numbers in time to control the pest. Before mass-rearing and augmentative release programs are initiated, it is necessary to know the true value of the various beneficials in controlling the pests.

Biological pest management is the use of living organisms to maintain pest populations below damaging levels. The biological control method involves the use of living organisms, which act as the predators for the pests and harmful insects. The main advantage of the biological control method in the control of agricultural pests is that they are self-perpetuating.

Many pesticides kill beneficial insects as well as pests. Since pests tend to breed very fast, they will often come back first.

Biotechnical methods are highly specific since they influence either the behaviour or the development of the target pest and do not have direct biocide activity. They include semiochemicals (attractants and repellents used for mass trapping, lure and kill and mating disruption), sterile insect technique, growth regulators and antibiotics.

Alternative treatments

Olive fruit fly management

Managing fruit flies is a complex process and requires long-term sustained and planned activity. Semiochemical are used in monitoring systems as one of the most effective methods for the detection and quantification of pests. Additionally, mass trapping programs using traps with food baits are also effective in managing and reducing the population levels and pest pressure, keeping them at a tolerable level.

Monitoring is an ongoing survey which can be used to indicate the presence or absence of pests and whether their numbers are increasing or decreasing.

Lures. Monitoring employs the use of specific lures (para-pheromones) which are attractants to male fruit flies. Different lures attract different fruit fly species.

It is important that the insecticide used is fast acting to ensure that the fly is caught within the trap and killed.

Trap types. In combination with the various lures there are several different trap types available, including Lynfield, McPhail and Biotraps to name a few. While each trap type has its own features, most follow a similar principle using a dispenser for an appropriate lure and a fast-acting contact insecticide.

Lure and kill techniques. These act by attracting the fly to a location and then killing it via an insecticide or other method. A trap in this instance is not essential as the objective is to kill the flies, not to trap them for monitoring purposes.

Protein bait spray. Protein is essential for the development of fruit flies and is required before sexual maturity is reached. Protein sources are a good attractant for both males and females, and when combined with an insecticide can be a very effective control option. Commercial protein products are available in varying formulations including gels, pastes and liquids and should be applied at least weekly and reapplied after rainfall events. Protein sprays may cause fruit burn, so caution should be exercised in application.

Male Annihilation Technique (MAT). This uses a combination of an insecticide and a parapheramone to kill male flies, like monitoring, however this uses a block of absorbent material instead of a trap. MAT blocks need to be replaced every few months depending upon weather, to ensure that the insecticide remains effective.

MAT is more effective when used in combination with protein bait spraying.

Mass trapping uses a high density of traps to reduce a pest population. Commonly mass trapping uses wet-based traps in which flies drown, combined with protein, ammonia or other food-based volatile attractants, although dry traps may also be used. Mass traps need to be cleared regularly to reduce the build-up of dead flies and to limit attractiveness to non-target insects. Although not employed as often, sticky traps may also be considered a mass-trapping tool.

Trapping the olive fruit fly must be carried out preventively as this usually saves on the number of necessary treatments with insecticides.

Make your own olive fruit fly traps. The most common preparation is a mixture of water, vinegar and sugar, which is poured into a plastic bottle with a pierced hole. Attracted by the smell, flies enter but cannot escape, drowning in the mixture.

Traps with water and chickpeas or Torula yeast tablets dissolved in water are very effective as bait.

Protein trap with water and chickpeas.

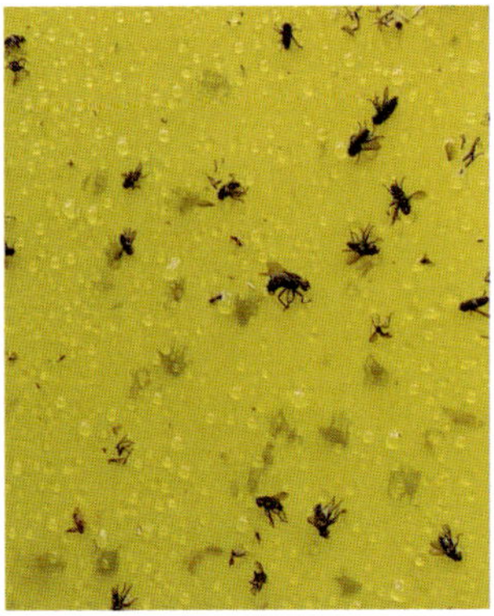

Olive fruit flies on a sticky card trap.

Sharpshooters on a sticky card trap.

Sexual attractants. Yellow sticky traps are baited with a sex pheromone (spiroketal) and/or ammonium bicarbonate attractant. The sex pheromone attracts the males whereas ammonium bicarbonate attracts both males and females. Both lures can be combined in one trap.

The spiroketal lures should be changed every four to six months and ammonium bicarbonate packets every two to six weeks. The flies should be removed weekly when the traps are monitored. Read the instructions carefully about how to handle and place the bait and pheromone.

Insecticide. Spinosad, a naturally derived insecticide produced by fermentation of the actinomycete *Saccharopolyspora spinosa,* can be an alternative to synthetic insecticides. It is effective for low-density populations of olive fruit fly.

Sanitation. Pick up and destroy fallen fruit to reduce olive fruit fly populations. Remove fruit as soon as possible once it is ripe to prevent the maggots from leaving the fruit and entering the soil to pupate. After harvest, collect all olive fruit left on trees or on the ground.

Biological Control. Some naturally occurring parasites are known to attack olive fruit fly, but they do not appear to provide adequate control.

Future focus: olive fruit fly management

Tools to combat olive fruit fly are in continual development. Some examples include:

Sterile Insect Technique (SIT). Future opportunities include the use of SIT as a pest suppression tool and options for commercial availability.

Biological controls including parasitoids (as well as augmentoria), nematodes, viruses and other entomopathogens, and biopesticides offer significant opportunities for increasing our fruit fly management toolbox.

Synthetic biology and genetic tools. Examples include ribonucleic acid interference (rNAI), gene drives and derivatives, although social licence concerns need to be addressed before wide-scale employment of such tools.

Digital tools. Smart traps, farm-based modelling and decision-support tools will help to improve monitoring and management responses and will greatly assist on-farm controls.

Novel chemistry including the development of new pesticides and importantly lures to attract fruit flies.

Plant breeding for crop varieties less susceptible or resistant to fruit-fly damage.

Glassy-winged sharpshooter management

- **Monitoring.** Check host plants for wilting foliage and dehydrated stems. Early detection and reporting are key elements in controlling Glassy-winged sharpshooter.
- **Traps.** In commercial settings, insect traps – for example, yellow sticky cards – can be used to monitor for sharpshooters.
- **Biological Control.** A healthy population of beneficial insects is the single most effective way to control sharpshooters. One of the most effective is a small wasp that feeds on the pest's egg masses. Praying mantises, assassin bugs and lacewings are also extremely beneficial at managing glassy-winged sharpshooters.

Apple weevil management

Traps consist of bands of acrylic fibres wrapped around the trunks of olive trees to obstruct crawling insects – especially the weevil – from climbing up the tree, damaging the soft leaves and hindering the plant's development. The insects, black and nocturnal, catch their feet in the acrylic fibres of the trap and can't move; the daytime sun then kills them.

Bands of acrylic fibres wrapped around the trunks of olive trees entangle climbing weevils.

Brown marmorated stink bug management

Tests for a rotating live trap for adult stink bugs was conducted in Italy with traps consisting of aggregation pheromone-baited cylinders with a wind vane, with the upwind end covered by mesh and the downwind end sealed by a removable entry-only mesh cone, admitting the attracted bugs. The DEAD-INN Stink Bug Trap uses pheromone technology.

Black scale management

Chemical control. If scale populations are high and there are few signs of parasitisation, an oil application may be employed to manage black scale. Application timing is crucial because insecticides are effective only against the crawlers (the most sensitive stage of the olive scale). Therefore, spraying applications should take place when crawlers emerge. One can use traps to determine when crawlers are hatching.

A narrow-range mineral oil, applied at high spray volumes (beyond the point of run-off), may be utilised to manage black scale. A recent study also suggests that canola oil (1 per cent by volume) may be utilised as a non-petroleum-based product to manage black scale on olives. Oil essentially suffocates the insect and is most effective at the crawler stage (early first instar); therefore, monitoring of the insect population is essential for successful control.

To properly time an oil application, double-sided sticky traps can be suspended in the tree canopy to monitor for presence of crawlers.

Use a hand lens to identify the crawlers; they will stick to the tape and look like tiny yellow dots. Oil applications must be completed before the insect enters the rubber stage or adult stage; thereafter, applications aren't effective.

Biological Control. Efficacy of biological control for management of black scale may vary by region.

A number of parasitoids (tiny wasps, barely visible to the naked eye) may attack black scale, including *Scutellista caerulea* and *Metaphycus helvolus,* providing effective control in many landscapes. General predators such as lacewings and ladybirds also feed on black scale.

Biological control of soft scales can often be inhibited by the activities of ants, which protect them from natural enemies.

Ant control is required where growers are interested in pursuing biological control, as ants harvest honeydew from black scale, and protect the scale from parasites and predators.

Manage them by circling trunks with a sticky material placed on trunk wraps to prevent ants from moving from the ground or infested plants to vegetation above the sticky barrier. Ant baits may also be effective. Potassium carbonate and potassium bicarbonate are foliar nutrients that may have incidental contact agent pest control properties.

Olive lace bug management

Olive trees are able to resist an attack by olive lace bugs and three most important areas to focus on are:

- Tree health.
- Spotting olive lace bugs early in the spring.
- Early and effective use of insecticide sprays.
  - **Cultural control.**

Good soil nutrition: Look carefully at soil and leaf analyses and deal with any significant deficits. Start the plant biology working so the trees look healthy with a dense leaf colour. Chemically treated soils produce weaker plants that are more physiologically stressed and these plants become more susceptible to disease and insect damage as well.

Magnesium and leaf chlorophyll: Chlorophyll is the stuff in the leaves, which makes photosynthesis possible. It is vital for tree health and damage by olive lace bug attack causes the leaves to turn yellow. Magnesium builds chlorophyll and helps the tree to resist olive lace bug attack. So look hard at the soil analysis and work on the Ca:Mg balance. Growers may have to spread some dolomite to raise the Mg content.

- **Chemical control.** In general, treatments for lace bugs are most effective when started during spring and early summer, when the season's first generation of nymphs is developing. Treatment should continue through the summer to combat subsequent generations.

  The olive lace bug is difficult to control as it feeds and breeds on the underside of the leaf, and it also multiplies prolifically. Good spray coverage is essential. The trick is to apply the sprays thoroughly to the undersides of leaves, where lace bugs feed and reproduce, in order to kill active populations of lace bug adults and larvae. It is important to apply insecticide soon after lace bug activity is first noticed, as populations can build up rapidly if left unchecked. Usually two sprays are required, as the first spray in spring will not kill the eggs, spray again in 10–14 days, and three or four sprays may be needed in total, depending on the area. Sometimes spraying with approved chemicals fails because rain washes off the chemical into the soil. Insecticides will not restore an undamaged appearance, but can reduce or prevent further damage.
- **Biological control.** Natural enemies of lace bugs include parasitic wasps, predatory assassin bugs, lacewing larvae, ladybirds, jumping spiders, pirate bugs and mites.

Verticillium tree management

There is no way to eradicate the infection from a tree, although the tree can be nursed along with reduced watering and nitrate fertilisers, pruning and balanced nutrition.

Inoculum levels can be reduced before planting by fumigating the soil, soil solarisation, pruning, burning and replacing the affected olive trees with resistant varieties or rootstocks. Avoid crushing the remains of infected branches. Avoid handling soil contaminated by the fungus (ploughing the olive groves helps to expand the *Verticillium dahliae* fungus).

- **Cultural control.** Recent studies start shedding light into the nutritional imbalances upon *V. dahliae* infection in olives, where potassium deficiency was found to increase the progress of olive-wilt disease. Similarly, recent trials with foliar and root application phosphonate salt copper phosphite (CuPh), which stimulates plant immunity and has antimicrobial properties, show some potential in olive trees.

- Plant resistant olive varieties and don't overwater trees.
- **Biological Control.** Other strategies for *V. dahliae* control currently being evaluated in olives are the application of beneficial microbes including *Aureobasidium pullulans* AP08 and *Bacillus amyloliquefaciens* PAB-024.

Peacock spot (olive leaf spot) management

- **Cultural control.** Peacock spot on olive tree leaves affects more plantations with excess nitrogen compared to others with good potassium nutrition. Hence, the need for a more rational and sustainable use of nitrogen fertilisers.

  The use of olive cultivars resistant to peacock spot is the most effective control method.
- **Chemical control.** Application of copper-based fungicides is the main method to control peacock spot disease. The best fungicide against olive leaf spot will depend on the time of application. Peacock spot is best managed by applying a preventive copper spray in late autumn. A second application in late winter is also recommended in areas subject to warm winters and spring rainfall.

  Note: Never apply copper fungicide on very hot days. Never mix copper fungicides with other chemicals. Never over-apply fungicides.

  According to the regulation 2009/1107 of the European Commission, copper compounds are included in the list of substances which are candidates for substitution as they are persistent in soil and toxic for the environment. The allowed quantity of copper has been progressively reduced to 28 kg per hectare over a period of seven years and its authorisation will expire on 31 December 2025 (European Commission implementing regulation 2018/1981).

Anthracnose management

Anthracnose is difficult to control once it has infected highly susceptible cultivars and some *Colletotrihum* species seem more resistant to copper fungicide, for example, *C. godetiae* is more resistant to copper than *C. nymphaeae*. Also, the recurrent application of copper-based fungicides (the main fungicides used in olive orchards) could drive the differences among *Colletotrichum* species based on their resistance.

Anthracnose fruit rot management should focus on preventing initial biotrophic infections by protecting olives during weather conditions that favour infection.

It is necessary to spray with copper as a preventive treatment before the fungus has a chance to penetrate the fruit. Spraying will not help cure infected fruits, but it will help stop the spread of the disease through the olive grove.

- The critical phases for disease control are during flowering and fruit set, and after harvest.

  The anthracnose fungus overwinters as mycelium and conidia on infected mummified fruits, twigs and leaves. The best strategy is to prevent the spread of disease from infected shoots, twigs and mummified fruits before spores are dispersed on flower buds and flowers in early spring. An early season application of protective fungicides is a key factor for successful management of anthracnose.

Chemical control of the disease

- Fungicide application focuses on reducing damage to the inflorescence from latent infection by the pathogen. Application of strobilurin-based fungicides at the pre-flowering stage, better if in combination with mancozeb, has been crucial in reducing the incidence of anthracnose in latent infections. In areas where anthracnose shows recurrent epidemic outbreaks and environmental conditions are conducive to the disease (mild temperature and high rainfall during the spring and autumn), the use of systemic fungicides to counteract primary infections on flowers and latent infections is necessary. The use of mancozeb or copper fungicides at veraison to control secondary infections should be driven by the weather conditions and the conduciveness to the disease outbreaks.

  The frequency of sprays is dictated by weather, region (climatic conditions), history of diseases and current disease incidence, variety and other factors.

  It is important to achieve good spray coverage with an appropriate fungicide. Complete coverage of large, tall trees is difficult to achieve; spraying is not very efficient and might not be justified or possible.

  Regular spraying of trees from pre-flowering time onwards with fungicides (at recommended label rates every 14 days) is useful to reduce the level of infection in the developing fruit.

  While control might occur in some situations, anthracnose can return annually and warrant a continued, preventive spray program. If anthracnose becomes serious in green immature fruit it would be useful to give a couple of judicious fungicide sprays.

Chemical control of pests

- Pests such as olive fruit fly and stink bugs make wounds in the olive that facilitate the entry and development of the fungus. Therefore, effective control of these insect pests is essential in the fight against the disease. Pest damage results in yield loss and higher spraying cost.

Cultural control

- Prune infected trees to increase air circulation and remove diseased twigs and branches. Destroy or dispose of diseased twigs and branches after pruning.
- The use of olive cultivars resistant to anthracnose is the most effective control method.

Stages of Integrated Pests and Disease Management (IPDM)

IPDM must be based on a sound knowledge of the pests and their natural enemies, diseases, action levels and management strategies. The most effective pest and disease management is achieved via a combination of methods, including prevention, observation and intervention.

Grove Management Best Practice

Prevention

Preventive cultural practices:

- Selecting varieties suited to local growing conditions.
- Maintaining healthy crops.
- Plant quarantine (plant sanitation, biosecurity).

Observation and Investigation problems

- Identification of diseases, pests and natural enemies.
- Monitoring: Inspection (regular observation is the cornerstone of IPM) of diseases and pests to work out the best time to apply pesticides.
- Use of on-farm weather stations to monitor and identify high-risk weather conditions (disease prediction models).

Intervention

- Biological control.
  - Mass release of beneficial organisms such as entomopathogenic fungus, competitors and antagonists.
  - Encourage presence of beneficial organisms in the grove by providing suitable habitat – use of cover crops.
- Biotechnical methods.
  - Sterile insect technique.
  - Mass trapping, barriers and film sprays.
- Cultural methods.
  - Including cultivars, agronomic techniques such as pruning, fertilisation, irrigation and soil management.

1. Cultivars

- The best way to prevent the onset of disease is to plant varieties that are resistant to the major pathogens in your area.

2. Fertiliser application – soil health and tree nutrition

Maintain good soil and tree health (happy trees).

Maintain the productive capacity of the soil without detriment to the environment.

- Manage application of fertilisers to optimise plant uptake and minimise losses to run-off, leaching or gas emissions.
- Undertake regular soil testing and leaf analysis.
- Understand fertiliser application methods – foliar, fertigation, broadcasting.
- Improve soil biology and build soil carbon through the application of compost, which can include grove and processing waste.
- Build soil nitrogen – nitrogen fixation.
- Use soil amendments (gypsum, sulphur and lime) to correct sodic (alkali) and acidic soils.
- Use non-chemical weed control options, for example mulches, cover crops, grazing, cultivation, flame and steam weeding.

3. Irrigation – water use

Be a responsible and efficient user of water:

- Understand olive tree water requirements (understand tree physiology).
- Undertake continuous monitoring of soil moisture and evaporation (application of remote sensing).
- Improve soil moisture infiltration, holding capacity and drainage properties.
- Maintain soil cover (plants/mulch) to manage soil temperature, conserve soil moisture and minimise water stress on the olive tree.
- Understand irrigation systems and design (micro-irrigation, sprinklers, furrow).
- Understand water trading and how to secure a water license.
- Set annual water-use targets.
- Understand and measure water use efficiency (litres of water per kilogram of product).

4. Canopy management – pruning

- Maintain a productive tree canopy.
- Undertake pruning to obtain optimal canopy surface to volume ratio, in accordance with your method of harvest.
- Undertake maintenance pruning to manage biennial bearing and achieve optimal light penetration and air flow (which also assists with effective spray coverage).

- Undertake renovation pruning on older trees to lower tree height, reduce wood and open up the canopy to sunlight to generate new fruiting wood.
- Monitor grove temperatures and implement frost and severe heat event mitigation strategies.

5. Orchard slashing – farm waste

Aim to minimise farm waste:

- Ensure appropriate use, recovery and disposal of processing waste.
- Convert organic waste to value-added products such as compost.

6. Better design of production systems to minimise pest problems

- Selection of appropriate olive cultivars resistant to pests, diseases and frost; planting density and canopy architecture.
- Change management practices to minimise the spread of pests and diseases – for example, harvest timing and hygienic pruning practices. Disinfect harvesting machines and pruning tools. Any tools (including chainsaws and woodchippers) that come into contact with infected wood should be sanitised before using on uninfected trees. Tools and equipment such as harvesters and bins can carry pests and weed seeds, so take particular care to inspect and clean them, especially if they are borrowed or were purchased second-hand.

  All parts of a vehicle can carry pests, so it is important that any vehicles that need access to growing areas are washed thoroughly before entering.
- Practice good grove hygiene, maintain quarantine and biosecurity best practice.

7. Use of selective (targeted) pesticides

A healthy tree is the best way to fight pests and diseases. However, on cultivars susceptible to pests and diseases spraying is a key part of combatting pests when they appear (timing and type of application of fungicides).

- Spray coverage, water volume and speed are affected by the canopy size of trees. Growers must calibrate the spraying equipment in order to achieve the optimum coverage required for the product/pest/disease.
- Action threshold is an important parameter, defined as the density at which control measures should be applied to prevent an increasing pest population from reaching the economic injury level. Once action is taken, follow up on its results by further monitoring, and by post-harvest assessment of fruit and oil yield and quality.
- The disease/pest cycle plays an important role in working out strategies for effective and timely management and in reducing the number of unnecessary applications of fungicides.
- Spot spraying – strategically timed and applied to a limited area to target pests and diseases.
- Implement chemical resistance strategies by rotating chemical groups as recommended.

- Consider use of narrow-spectrum (selective) pesticides.
- Consider use of pesticides which disrupt pest development or behaviour, for example pheromones, insect growth regulators and oil sprays.
- Consider use of natural or organic control methods (although these are not always the least disruptive choice).

8. Spraying – agricultural chemical management

Practice responsible management by minimising agri-chemical use while also protecting the industry from pests and diseases.

- Be aware of relevant national and state government legislative requirements for the use of agri-chemicals.
- Mitigate agrichemical risks and safety hazards:
  - Ensure persons applying chemicals use protective clothing and are trained and licensed as required by national and state legislation.
  - Ensure agri-chemicals are safely and securely stored on farm.
  - Ensure correct disposal of used chemical containers, and unwanted chemicals.
- Read the label – always use chemicals in accordance with label and permit approvals – target pests, spray dilution, application rates and withholding periods (to meet MRL requirements).
- Maintain a chemical-use inventory or spray-diary record (paper or electronic).
- Maintain an up-to-date file of APVMA Permits, Product Labels and Material Safety Data Sheets (MSDS) for all agri-chemicals used in your grove(s).
- Minimise off-target impact – avoid spraying in unsuitable weather conditions (follow wind speed restrictions) and observe buffer zones around sensitive crops, water courses and nature reserves.
- Ensure that spray application equipment is regularly calibrated for optimal droplet size and delivery rate.
- Make sure the withholding period has passed before picking treated fruit and be sure to wash them well before eating. Insecticide sprays can be harmful if used incorrectly, so always read and follow the label directions.

IPDM Attributes

IPM must be effective and so there are several criteria to evaluate:

- Effectiveness in controlling pest populations.
- Cost of treatment.
- Human and non-target-animal toxicity.
- Environmental persistence.
- Quality of product.

Food Quality Plan (olive oil and table fruits)

- Ensure all withholding periods have been observed (chance of chemical residues on the olives if the sprays have not been applied correctly; chance of chemicals being used that do not have APVMA certification).
- Ensure all chemicals have approved on-label use or APVMA permits (avoid chemical residue on olives).
- Ensure the olives do not have significant spoilage due to fungal or insect damage. High-quality olive oil requires olives that are not contaminated with anthracnose, sooty mould spores or insects.
- Ensure good nutrition plant practices. An imbalance of nutrients in the soil or on the foliage could affect the cell structure of the olives, compromising the quality of the fruit and increasing susceptibility to pests and diseases.
- Ensure good irrigation practices. If irrigation is used on an olive grove a good understanding of the growth cycle of the trees will be required to schedule this irrigation. Olives with too high a water content can cause problems at the mill at the point of extraction.
- Frost, flood, drought and fire impact on grove productivity and can also impact on product quality – monitor and manage these risks where possible. The 'frosted' defect is characteristic of oils extracted from olives that have been injured by pre-harvest frost. Aromas, such as stewed fruit, fresh-cut mushrooms, wet wood, sweet aroma, bitterness and pungency, tend to disappear and the fruit flavours 'muddle' – they are not crisp and clear.

GENERAL GUIDELINES

The following guidelines are based on the Australian Standard AS 2507-1998 for 'Minor Storage' of farm chemicals.

- All pesticides and veterinary medicines must be stored out of reach of children, pets, livestock and unauthorised people in a locked, secure facility. All doors and windows should be secure. Only authorised people with appropriate training and/or experience in chemical handling should have access to store keys.
- Chemicals should be stored in the original containers with labels intact and material safety data sheets should be kept in a register nearby. If labels come off, always re-label the container with the proper product label. Regularly check containers for leaks. Replace old leaking containers with containers of similar size and construction as previously used to store the same chemical. Never store chemicals in food or drink containers.
- Store chemicals away from personal protective equipment. Such equipment should be stored near, but not in, the store.
- Keep pesticides separate from fertilisers, animal feeds, seeds and other non-agricultural chemicals.

- Store chemicals in their separate chemical groups. For example, insecticides should be stored away from herbicides.
- Read storage directions on the label. Some products, such as Dipel, must be stored in a cool dry place.
- Powder or granular products should be placed above liquid products to prevent leakage into, and contamination of, powder/granular products.
- Store hazardous material on lower shelves to minimise splash, should the container fall.
- Always ensure chemical containers are properly sealed after use.
- Ensure spill containment materials, such as absorbent vermiculite or sand, are located close to the store.
- Avoid storing agricultural chemicals for more than one season.
- Maintain an inventory book of agricultural chemicals in the store.
- Safety procedures on mixing of chemicals and response to spillage should be available.

The Facility

The store should be a dedicated facility or room that is not used for any other purpose. Do not locate the store in an area prone to flooding.

Locate the store a safe distance – approximately 30m (100ft) is suggested, depending on land undulation – from buildings, work areas, watercourses, water bodies, drains, sewers and bores.

Locate the store in an open area with a low risk from bushfires.

A clean and reliable water supply should be close to the chemical store for tank-filling and emergency use. An emergency shower/eye wash facility is essential.

The storage facility should be well ventilated, allowing good air circulation to prevent the build-up of chemical vapours. Temperature extremes should be avoided. The storage facility should also be well lit to allow for easy reading of labels.

The floor should ideally be impervious to prevent environmental contamination in the event of a chemical spill. The store should be bonded (or a viable alternative can be used, such as storing the chemical container in a container of larger volume) to contain chemical spills.

The facility should be of sound construction to resist wind and withstand weather damage and be leak-proof and vermin-proof.

Signage

Provide the following signage at entry points: 'Pesticide store', 'Authorised staff only', 'No smoking'. Inside, have the signage: 'No smoking'.

Phytosanitary

Organisms that are very dangerous to plants are called quarantine harmful plant organisms, which are generally of foreign type and may cause major damage for the economy, society and the environment in areas where they were not present before. Early detection of quarantine harmful plant organisms and new potentially dangerous diseases and pests is crucial for taking rapid and efficient action and immediate eradication in the event of their occurrence or outbreak.

A quarantine pest (for example, insects, mites, nematodes, phytoplasms, bacteria, fungi, viruses and viroids) is a pest of potential economic importance to the area endangered thereby and not yet present there, or present but not widely distributed and being officially controlled.

Phytosanitary legislation involves government laws that are essential to minimise the risk of the introduction and diffusion of pests, especially invasive non-native species, as a consequence of the international exchange of plant material, thus allowing to safeguard agricultural production and biodiversity of a territory.

Phytosanitary (plant health) certificates are issued to indicate that consignments of plants, plant products or other regulated articles meet specified phytosanitary import or export requirements and are in conformity with the certifying statement of the appropriate model certificate.

Early detection of exotic pests and diseases is crucial in order to stop their spread.

Making olive groves green again. (BORJA JIMÉNEZ-ALFARO, UNIVERSITY OF OVIEDO)

CHAPTER 5

Biodiversity and Beneficials

Biodiversity is the basis for the environmental health of our planet and the source of economic, ecological and food security for future generations.

Biodiversity is all the different kinds of life you'll find in one area – the variety of animals, insects, plants, fungi and bacteria. Each of these species and organisms work together in ecosystems, like an intricate web, to maintain balance and support life.

Pests and diseases are also part of the natural environmental system. Unfortunately, most people are more aware of the few insects that cause problems than they are of the many beneficial insects. In this system there is a balance between predators and pests. This is nature's way of controlling populations.

Why is insect Biodiversity important?

Insects suppress pests, reducing chemical use, pollinate crops and help to build healthy soils.

Insects develop important functional roles in terrestrial ecosystems as herbivores, pollinators, decomposers, predators, parasites and food for wildlife.

How insects help biodiversity?

They cycle nutrients, pollinate plants, disperse seeds, maintain soil structure and fertility, control populations of other organisms, and provide a major food source for other taxa.

The olive-grove environment and natural biodiversity

Olive groves and their surrounding environment make up an ecosystem where numerous species of all types coexist. Studies, including from the FAO (such as *The state of the world's biodiversity for food and agriculture, 2019*), have determined that olive plantations can support up to 200 wild plant species, 90 vertebrates and 160 invertebrate species per hectare.

Many invertebrate flora and fauna species depend on olive groves. These are the foundations of biodiversity. Many species of mammals, birds and reptiles are intricately linked to olive trees, including quail, partridges, owls, hoopoes and lizards, among many others. These animals find the food and shelter necessary for their survival in olive groves, underlining their importance for sustaining a great diversity of wildlife.

In the largest study conducted worldwide on the biodiversity of olive groves, researchers from the Spanish project Olivares Vivos confirmed their importance in terms of biodiversity.

Altogether, 180 species of birds, 60 species of ants, 200 species of wild bees and more than 750 species of plants were found in the 40 olive groves studied, including a new species of plant for science, *Linaria qartobensis*.

When olive groves are properly managed, and when the environmental sustainability of the area they are grown in is considered, they undoubtedly comprise one of the greatest artificial environments supporting natural biodiversity that exists today. They are beneficial not only to the economy, society and culture, but also to the surrounding environment.

Many people are quite unaware of the amazing wildlife that lives in olive groves.

Koala on an olive tree.

Kangaroo in an olive grove.

Owl in an olive tree. (SEO/BIRDLIFE)

Snake on an olive tree. (ENZO CARUSO)

Emus *(Dromaius novaehollandiae)* among olive trees in Australia.

Greater Rhea (*Rhea americana*) in an olive grove in Uruguay. (ANTONIO TRAPERO)

Bird's nest in an olive tree. (ROGER HARRISON)

Bird's nest with eggs in an olive tree.

Tree frogs (Hylidae) in Australia.

Jezebel butterfly in Australia. (ELLEN REID)

Water Dragon lizard in Australia under an olive tree. (ROGER HARRISON)

Echidna under an olive tree in Australia.

Water Dragon lizard in Australia. (MODERN OLIVES/BOUNDARY BEND)

Australian King-Parrot.

Case moth, *Clania ignobilis*, in Australia. The larvae normally only protrude the head and thorax out of the case, while the soft abdomen is kept inside.

Male Iberian lynx, *Lynx pardinus*, in Spain. (TODOLIVO)

Chameleon on an olive tree in Portugal. (S. HENRIQUES)

Horse in an olive grove in Croatia.

Beneficial insects – predators, parasites and pollinators

There is a huge array of beneficial, including hoverflies, lacewings, parasitic wasps, predatory wasps, ladybirds, predatory mites, spiders, ground beetles, and the list goes on. Every country is rich in insect life and has many unique species.

Growers may not realise it, but many bugs are good for olive groves. We call these 'beneficial bugs', and they help by eating pest insects that want to eat your plants. Your olive grove has thousands of insects, and of them, most are either beneficial or harmless.

'Beneficial bugs' are classified into three main categories:

1. Pollinators – Bugs such as butterflies, moths, and bees pollinate the flowers, thereby contributing to proliferation or reproduction.
2. Predators – Bugs such as praying mantises, ladybirds, ground beetles, lacewings, syrphid (hover) flies, aphid midges (Aphidoletes) and yellowjacket wasps eliminate pests by eating them.
3. Parasitisers – Bugs such as parasitic wasps lay their eggs inside or on the pests. After hatching, the larvae eat or feed on the host insects and kill them or debilitate their host. They are relatively specific to certain insect groups.

What do beneficial insects do?

In general, beneficial insects control the pest populations by feeding on them. Thereby, they protect the main crops and increase their commercial value.

Bees [Hymenoptera: Apidae]

- European honey bee, *Apis mellifera*

Nest of feral bees with wax combs on a branch of an olive tree. (SHANE ROYAN)

Ladybirds [Coleoptera: Coccinellidae]

Harmonia octomaculata, H. conformis, H. axyridis, Coccinella novemnotata

Left: Ladybird on olive tree.
Right: Ladybird larva.

Mealybug ladybird [Coleoptera: Coccinellidae]

Cryptolaemus montrouzieri

C. montrouzieri feeding on soft scales. (JOE WESSELS)

C. montrouzieri feeds on all stages of mealybugs. (PLANET NATURAL)

Mealybug Ladybird has been identified as an effective biological control agent.

Soldier beetle [Coleoptera: Cantharidae]

Long-nosed lycid beetle
Porrostoma sp.

Long-nosed lycid beetle, *Porrostoma* species.

Spined predatory shield bug

Oechalia schellenbergii (Guérin) [Hemiptera: Pentatomidae]

Schellenberg soldier bug, *Oechalia schellenberg*, attacking larva of light brown apple moth.

Green lacewing

Mallada signata [Neuroptera: Chrysopidae]

In larval stages, lacewings are voracious and indiscriminate predators, consuming most soft-bodied insects including mites, aphids, beetle larvae, small caterpillars and eggs of a variety of species, thrips and immature whiteflies. Right: Lacewing larva. (WHITNEY CRANSHAW)

Green lacewing adult. (LESLEY WILSON)

Lacewing eggs. (NATHALIE BEAUCHAMP)

Robber flies [Diptera: Asilidae]

Robber fly.

Hover fly [Diptera: Syrphidae]

Hoverfly.

Hoverfly. (STEVE GOMBOCZ)

Praying mantis [Mantodea: Mantidae]

Praying mantises are predators, eating mostly insects but have been known to eat small vertebrates.

Praying mantis. (MICHAEL S. PRICE)

Praying mantis egg case (ootheca).

Praying mantis on an olive trunk. (FREEPIK)

Spiders [Araneae: Araneidae, Lycosidae, Oxyopidae, Salticidae, Thomisidae]

Two of the many spider species found in olive trees.

Diaea evanida spider.

Egg sac of two-tailed spider.

Egg sacs of the *Ordgarius furcatus*, or the bolas spider.

Spider web and eggs.

Wasps

Parasitic wasp

[Hymenoptera: Braconidae, Ichneumonidae, Eulophidae, Aphelinidae, Trichogrammatidae, Vespidae, Scelionidae]

These wasps are a large and diverse group of parasitoids.

The Australian paper wasp is an important pollinator and contributor to the Australian ecosystem.

Trissolcus basalis is an important biocontrol agent of many pests. Females lay their eggs inside the eggs of their hosts. The larva hatches and completely consumes the host embryo, eventually emerging as an adult. This image shows *Trissolcus basalis* on a Brown marmorated sting bug egg mass. (CHARUWAT TAEKUL)

Metaphycus dispar is a parasite of soft scale. (MUSI-AKASHI.COCOLOG)

APPENDIX I

List of Olive Pests

Olive fruit fly *Bactrocera oleae* (Rossi, 1790)

Queensland fruit fly *Bactrocera tryoni* (Froggatt, 1897)

Mediterranean fruit fly *Ceratitis capitata* (Wied, 1824)

Olive leaf gall midge *Dasineura oleae* (Angelini, 1831) = *Perrisia oleae*

Olive fruit midge *Lasioptera berlesiana* (Paoli, 1907) = *Prolasioptera berlesiana*, *L. brevicornis*

Olive bark midge / Olive shoot midge *Resseliella oleisuga* (Targioni-Tozzetti, 1887)

Olive moth *Prays oleae* (Bernard, 1788)

Moth *Zelleria oleastrella* (Milliere, 1864)

Olive Pyralid Moth *Euzophera pinguis* (Haworth, 1811)

Jasmine moth or palpita *Palpita unionalis* (Hübner, 1796) = *Palpita vitrealis* (Rossi, 1794) = *Margaronia unionalis* (Hb)

Olive leaf moth *Palpita forficifera* (Munroe, 1959)

Olive leaf moth/Olive shootworm *Palpita persimilis* (Munroe, 1959)

Lilac pyralid *Palpita nigropunctalis* (Bremer, 1864)

Moth *Argyrotaenia sphaleropa* (Meyrick, 1909)

Light brown apple moth *Epiphyas postvittana* (Walker, 1863)

European grapevine moth *Lobesia botrana* (Denis and Schiff, 1776)

Rustic sphinx moth *Manduca rustica* (Fabricius, 1775)

Privet hawkmoths

- *Psilogramma menephron* (Cramer, 1780)
- *Psilogramma casuarinae* (Walker)

Death's head hawkmoth *Acherontia atropos* (Linnaeus, 1758)

Leopard moth / wood-borer moth *Zeuzera pyrina* (Linnaeus, 1761)

Weevil / Olive fruit curculio *Rhynchites cribripennis* (Desbrochers, 1869)

Olive borer, Olive bark beetle, Barrenillo negro *Hylesinus oleiperda* (Fabricius, 1792)

Apple weevil *Otiorhynchus cribricollis* (Gyllenhal, 1834)

Garden weevil *Phlyctinus callosus* (Boheman, 1834)

Olive weevil *Dyscerus perforatus* (Roelofs, 1873)

Olive bark beetle *Phleotribus scarabeoides* (Bernard, 1788) = *P. oleae* (Latr)

South American fruit tree weevil

- *Naupactus xanthographus* (Germar, 1824)
- *Pantomorus cervinus* (Boheman, 1840)

Fuller's rose weevil *Pantomorus cervinus* (Boheman, 1840)

Powderpost beetles / Tree wood-borers

- *Dexicrates robustus* (Blanchard, 1851)
- *Neoterius mystax* (Blanchard, 1851)

Common auger beetle *Xylopsocus gibbicollis* (MacLeay, 1873)

Twig pruner *Cloniocerus kraussii* (White, 1855)

Olive flea beetles

- *Agropistes oleae* (Bryant, 1922)
- *A. capensis* (Bryant)

- *A. sexittatus* (Bryant)

African black beetle *Heteronychus arator* (Fabricius, 1775)

Cockchafer *Melolontha papposa* (Illiger, 1803)

Beetles/White grubs

- *Holotrichia longipennis* (Blanch, 1851)
- *Anomala polita* (Blanch, 1851)

White-spotted rose beetle *Oxythyrea funesta* (Poda, 1761)

Blister beetle *Hycleus pustulatus* (Thunberg, 1821) = *Mylabris pustulata* (Olivier, 1795)

Spanish fly *Lytta vesicatoria* (Linnaeus, 1758)

Eriophyd mites

- *Aceria oleae* (Nalepa, 1900)
- *Oxycenus maxwelli* (Keifer, 1939)
- *Aculus olearius* (Castagnoli, 1977)
- *Aceria olivi* (Zaher and Abou-Awad, 1979)
- *Aculops benakii* (Hatzinikolis, 1969)
- *Tegonotus oleae* (Natcheff, 1966)
- *Oxycenus niloticus* (Zaher and Abou-Awad, 1979)
- *Tegolophus hassani* (Keifer, 1959)
- *Ditrymacus athiasellus* (Keifer, 190)
- *Shevtchenkella barensis* (Vidovic and Petanovic, 2008)

Olive gall mite *Aceria oleae*

Olive bud mite *Oxycenus maxwelli*

Olive rust mite *Tegolophus hassani*

Thrips

Aeolothripidae

- *Aeolothrips collaris* (Priesner, 1919)
- *Aeolothrips intermedius* (Bagnall, 1934)
- *Franklinothrips megalops* (Trybom, 1912)

Melanthripidae

- *Melanthrips fuscus* (Sulzer, 1776)

Thripidae

- *Frankliniella occidentalis* (Pergande, 1895)
- *Frankliniella schultzei* (Trybom, 1910)
- *Thrips imagines* (Bagnall, 1926)
- *Frankliniella occidentalis* (Pergande, 1895)
- *Neohydatothrips amygdali* (Minaei, 2016)
- *Thrips tabaci* (Lindeman, 1889)

Phlaeothripidae

- *Liothrips oleae* (Costa, 1857)
- *Haplothrips andresi* (Priesner, 1931)
- *Haplothrips tritici* (Kurdjumov, 1912)

Soft scales

- Black scale *Saissetia oleae* (Olivier, 1791)
- Hemispherical scale *Saissetia coffeae* (Walker, 1852)
- Brown soft scale *Coccus hesperidum* (Linnaeus, 1758)
- Viburnum/Cushion scale *Lichtensia viburni* (Signoret, 1873)
- Carinated cottony scale *Filippia follicularis* (Targ, 1867) = *Fillipia oleae* (Costa, 1857)
- *Metaceronema japonica* (Maskell, 1897)

Armoured (hard) scales

- Oleander scale *Aspidiotus nerii* (Bouché, 1833)
- Violet scale *Parlatoria oleae* (Colvée, 1880)
- *Lepidosaphes destefanii* (Leonardi, 1907) = *L. flava* (Signoret, 1870)
- Oystershell/Mussel scale *Lepidosaphes ulmi* (Linnaeus, 1758)
- Red scale *Aonidiella aurantii* (Maskell, 1879)
- Greedy scale *Hemiberlesia rapax* (Comstock, 1881)
- *Leucaspis riccae* (Targ, 1881)
- *Pseudaulacaspis pentagona* (Targ, 1886)
- San Jose scale *Quadraspidiotus perniciosus* (Com, 1881), *Q. lenticularis* (Lind, 1912), *Q. maleti* (Bal, 1950) = *Diaspidiotus maleti* (Vays, 1920)
- *Melanaspis corticosa* (Brain, 1919)

- Ross scale (araucaria black scale; round black scale) *Lindingaspis rossi* (Maskell, 1892)
- Circular black scale *Chrysomphalus aonidum* (Linnaeus, 1758)
- Latania scale *Hemiberlesia lataniae* (Signoret, 1869)

Ornate, pit olive scale *Pollinia pollini* (Costa, 1857)

Ensign scale *Orthezia olivicola* (Beingolea, 1965) = *Praelongorthezia olivicola* (Kozar, 2004)

Mealybugs

- Long-tailed mealybug *Pseudococcus longispinus* (Targ-Toz, 1867)
- Obscure mealybug *Pseudococcus viburni* (Signoret, 1875)
- Cotton/Solanum mealybug *Phenacoccus solani* (Ferris, 1918)
- Mango mealybug Drosicha mangiferae (Steb, 1903)

Aphid *Prociphilus oleae* (Leach, 1826)

Brown marmorated stink bug *Halyomorpha halys* (Stål, 1855)

Green vegetable bug *Nezara viridula* (Linnaeus, 1758)

Green stink bug *Plautia affinis* (Dallas, 1851)

Leaf-footed bug *Leptoglossus phyllopus* (Linnaeus, 1767)

Olive psyllids

- *Euphyllura olivina* (Costa, 1839)
- *Euphyllura phillyreae* (Foerster, 1848)
- *Euphyllura pakistanica* (Loginova, 1973)

Olive whitefly

- *Aleurolobus olivinus* (Silvestri, 1911)
- *Siphoninus phillyreae* (Halliday, 1835)

Olive lace bug *Froggattia olivinia* (Froggatt, 1901)

Olive tingit (Lace bug)

- *Plerochila australis* (Distant, 1904)
- *Cysteochila lineata* (Rodrigues, 1982)
- *Neoplerochila paliatseasi* (Rodrigues, 1982)
- *Neoplerochila* sp.

Lace bug *Eteoneus sigillatus* (Drake and Poor, 1936)

Rutherglen bug *Nysius vinitor* (Bergroth, 1891)

Bug *Closterotomus trivialis* (Costa, 1853)

Barrillo *Hysteropterum grylloides* (Fabricius, 1794)

Spittlebug *Philaenus spumarius* (Linnaeus, 1758)

Glassy-winged sharpshooter *Homalodisca vitripennis* (Germar, 1821)

Cicadas [Hemiptera: Cicadidae]

- Redeye cicada *Psaltoda moerens* (Germar, 1834)
- Silver Knight or Black Prince cicada *Psaltoda plaga* (Walker, 1850)
- *Cicada orni* (Linnaeus, 1758),
- *Lyristes plebejus* (Scopoli, 1763)
- *Tibicen plebejus* (Scopoli, 1763)
- *Cicadetta brullei* (Fieber, 1876)
- *Psalmocharias plagifera* (Schum, 1922)

Katydids or bush crickets *Scudderia* sp.

Wingless grasshopper *Phaulacridium vittatum*

Olive seed wasp *Eupelmus spermophilus* (Silvestri, 1915)

Leaf-cutting ants

- *Acromyrmex crassispinus* (Forel)
- *Acromyrmex laticeps* (Emery)
- *Acromyrmex lundii* (Guérin)
- *Acromyrmex striatus* (Roger)
- *Acromyrmex ambiguus* (Emery)

Termites

APPENDIX II

List of Olive Diseases

FUNGAL DISEASES

Peacock spot

Fusicladium oleagineum (Castagne) Ritschel and U. Braun (syn. *Venturia oleaginea* (Castagne) Rossman and Crous, *Cycloconium oleaginum, Spilocaea oleagina* (Castagne))

Anthracnose or 'Soapy fruit'

Colletotrichum gloeosporioides (Penz.) Penz. and Sacc. in Penz. = *Gloeosporium olivarum* Almeida
Colletotrichum acutatum J. H. Simmonds
C. simmondsii, C. clavatum, C. alienum, C. boninense, C. fioriniae, C. fructicola, C. theobromicola, C. nymphaeae, C. godetiae, C. perseae

Cercosporiose

Pseudocercospora cladosporioides (Sacc.) U. Braun

Dalmatian disease

Botryosphaeria dothidea (Moug.) Cesati and De Notaris (= *Macrophoma dalmatica* (Thüm) Berl. and Voglino and *Sphaeropsis dalmatica* (Thüm.) Gigante = *Camarosporium dalmaticum* (Thüm.) Zachos and Tzav. Klon

Neofusicoccum (Botryosphaeria fruit rot)

Neofusicoccum luteum

Leprosy [Lepra]

Phlyctema vagabunda Desm. (syn: *Neofabraea alba*) and *Neofabraea vagabunda* or *Gloeosporium album*

Alternaria fruit rot

Alternaria alternata, A. solani, A. sp., *A. infectoria,*

Other fruit rots

Aspergillus niger, A. ochraceus
Aureobasidium pullulans
Arthrinium phaeospermum
Capnodium elaeophilum
Cladosporium herbarum, C. cladosporioides, C. herbarum
Diplodia seriata,
Fusarium lateritium, F. solani, F. nygamai, F. moniliforme, F. arthrosporioides/avenaceum
Pilidium concavum
Phomopsis sp.
Phytophthora nicotianae, P. oleae sp. *nov*
Epicoccum nigrum
Penicillium expansum, P. spp.
Stemphylium amaranthi
Rhizopus stolonifer
Trichothecium roseum
Trichoderma harzianum
Truncatella angustata

Branch cankers, dieback and leaf necrosis

Athelia rolfsii
Arthrinium phaeospermum
Biscogniauxia mediterranea
Biscogniauxia rosacearum
Botryosphaeria dothidea, B. ribis,
Cadophora luteo-olivacea,
Celerioriella umnquma sp. *nov.*
Coniothyrium ferrarisianum
Coniochaeta velutina, C. fasciculata
Cylindrocarpon destructans
Cytospora oleina, C. oleicola, C. olivarum, C. plurivora, C. sorbicola, C. pruinosa
Dactylonectria macrodidyma, D. torresensis, D. novozelandica, D. valentina
Diaporthe foeniculina, D. viticol
Diatrype oregonensis, D. stigma
Didymocyrtis banksiae
Diplodia mutila, D. seriata, Diplodia africana, D. fraxini, D. subglobosa
Didymosphaeria variabile
Dothiorella iberica, D. omnivora, D. sarmentorum, D. sempervirentis
Eutypa lata
Fomitiporella sp.
Fusarium solani, F. acuminatum F. eumartii, F. oxysporum, F. lateritium

Heterotruncatella sp.
Ilyonectria robusta, I. capensis
Lasiodiplodia theobromae
Neofabraea kienholzii
Neofusicoccum mediterraneum, N. luteum, N. parvum, N. vitifusiforme, N. australe, N. stellenboschiana
Neonectria radicicola
Neophaeomoniella niveniae
Phaeomoniella chlamydospora
Phaeoacremonium aleophilum, P. richardsiae, P. aleophilum, P. africanum, P. alvesii, P. italicum, P. minimum, P. oleae, P. parasiticum, P. prunicola, P. scolytii, P. spadicum, P. sicilianum, P. iranianum
Phoma incompta, P. cladoniicola
Phomopsis sp.
Phlyctema vagabunda
Pleurostoma richardsiae
Pleurostomophora richardsiae
Punctularia atropurpurascens
Pseudophaeomoniella globosa, P. oleae
Pythium schmitthenner, P. irregulare
Sardiniella urbana
Schizophyllum commune
Sclerotium rolfsii
Thelonectria aurea
Trametes versicolour
Ulocladium consortiale
Vredendaliella oleae
Xenocylindrosporium margaritarum sp. *nov*

Verticillium wilt
Verticillium dahliae Kleb.

Phytophthora root rot
Phytophthora acerina, P. cactorum, P. cinnamomi, P. citricola sensu lato, P. cryptogea, P. drechsleri, P. inundata, P. megasperma, P. nicotianae, P. oleae, P. palmivora, P. pini, P. plurivora, P. crassamura, P. niederhauserii, P. pseudocryptogea, P. bilorbang

Charcoal root rot
Macrophomina phaseolina (Tassi) Goidanich = *Sclerotium bataticola* Taubenh.

Rhizoctonia root rot
Rhizoctonia solani

Armillaria root rot
Armillaria mellea (Vahl:Fr.) Kumm.
Armillaria luteobubalina (Watling and Kile)

White root rot
Rosellinia necatrix Berl. ex Prill. (anamorph *Dematophora necatrix* R. Hartig)

Wood decay
Fomes fulvus var. *oleae* (Scop)
Fomitiporia mediterranea (Fisch)
Phellinus igniarius (L) Quél.
Polyporus spp.
Stereum hirsutum (Willd) S.F. Gray
Dactylonectria torresensis (A. Cabral, Rego and Crous)
Schizophyllum commune Fr.
Trametes versicolor (L.) Lloyd

Mushroom/Tree fungi
Omphalotus olearius (DC.) Singer
Omphalotus illudens (Schwein)
Massariella oleae (Corte)
Pycnoporus cinnabarinus (Jacquin) Karsten

Sooty moulds
Aureobasidium pullulans (De Bary) G. Arnaud
Capnodium elaeophilum Prill.
Limacinula spp.

BACTERIAL DISEASES

Olive knot
Pseudomonas savastanoi pv. *savastanoi* (Smith) Gardan *et al.*

Bacterial canker
Xanthomonas sp.

Crown gall
Agrobacterium tumefaciens (Smith and Townsend) Conn = *Rhizobium radiobacter*
Agrobacterium radiobacter (Beijerinck and van Delden)

Wound Canker
Xanthomonas campestris
Ralstonia solanacearum
Burkholderia caryophylli

Olive quick decline syndrome (OQDS)
Xylella fastidiosa subsp. *pauca* (Xfp)

PHYTOPLASMA DISEASES

Olive witches' brooms 'Stolbur' phytoplasma

VIRUS DISEASES and VIRUS-LIKE DISEASES

Olive leaf yellowing associated virus (OLYaV)
Cherry leaf roll virus (CLRV)

Arabis mosaic virus (ArMV)
Olive latent virus-1 (OLV-1)
Olive latent virus-2 (OLV-2)
Olive latent virus-3
Cucumber mosaic virus (CMV)
Strawberry latent ring spot virus (SLRSV)
Olive semi latent virus (OSLV)
Olive mild mosaic virus (OMMV)
Olive yellow mottling and decline associated virus (OYMDaV)
Olive latent ring spot virus (OLRSV)
Olive latent [Tepovirus: Betaflexiviridae] T (OlVT)
Olive vein yellow associated virus (OVYaV)
Tobacco necrosis virus D (TNV)
Tobacco mosaic virus (TMV)
Nepovirus: ArMV, CLRV, SLRSV, OLV1, OLRSV
Cucumovirus: CMV
Oleavirus: OLV2
Potexvirus: OYVV
Capillovirus: OYMDV
Tobamovirus: TMV
Tepovirus: T(OlVT)
Closterovirus: OLYV
Olive semi-latent virus (OSLV)

PARASITIC NEMATODES

Root decay
Tylenchulus semipenetrans Cobb

Root-knot nematode
Meloidogyne arenaria (Neal) Chitwood
M. hapla Chitwood
M. incognita (Kofoid and White) Chitwood
M. javanica (Treub) Chitwood

Root-lesion nematode
Pratylenchus penetrans (Cobb) Sher and Allen
P. vulnus Allen and Jensen

Root necrosis
Helicotylenchus sp.

INDEX

Published in 2024 by Reed New Holland Publishers
Sydney

Level 1, 178 Fox Valley Road, Wahroonga, NSW 2076, Australia

newhollandpublishers.com

Printed in China

A record of this book is held at the National Library of Australia.

ISBN 9781760796143

Managing Director: Fiona Schultz
Publisher and Project Editor: Simon Papps
Designer: Andrew Davies
Production Director: Arlene Gippert